your *organic*
allotment

your organic
allotment

Ian Spence

Pauline Pears

First published in Great Britain in 2007
by Gaia Books,
a division of Octopus Publishing Group Ltd
2–4 Heron Quays, London E14 4JP

ISBN-13: 978-185675-278-7
ISBN-10: 1-85675-278-X

A CIP catalogue record of this book is available
from the British Library.

Printed and bound in China

10 9 8 7 6 5 4 3 2 1

Always read the manufacturers' instructions
carefully before using any organic fertilizers,
biological controls or pesticides. All information
is accurate and all products mentioned are
available for purchase at the time of printing,
although we cannot guarantee that they will
remain available indefinitely.

contents

foreword

Lawrence Hills, founder of the Henry Doubleday Research Association, now known as Garden Organic, was a man ahead of his time. When I started work with him 25 years ago, the organic message he was promoting was seen as 'fringe' at best, dismissed as irrelevant by most. Farming and gardening had embraced chemical, artificial, growing methods wholeheartedly. Little could I have imagined then how much things would change. Organic growing is now the method of choice for a large, and increasing, number of food producers – amateur and professional – around the world, and demand for the produce increases every year.

To be sold as organic, produce must be grown in ways that conform to legally binding organic standards that cover all aspects of the way land and plants are treated. Obviously allotment growers have no need for legally binding standards, but the same principles and practices apply on this level, too. The organic methods described in this book conform to Garden Organic's Organic Gardening Guidelines, which are based on the standards for commercial growers.

The prime aim in organic growing is to maintain and improve the environment – both above and below ground – to promote healthy plant growth. The goal is long-term sustainability on your plot, and also in the wider environment, so methods and materials used reflect this. Recycling, reuse, local sourcing and user and environmentally friendly are all key concepts.

Organic standards have wildlife conservation as an essential part of the growing system. Organic growers rely on natural predators and parasites, such as ladybirds, hoverflies and birds, to keep pest and disease levels under control. Creating an environment that is attractive to wildlife is vital. This is why organic farms have been shown to have a richer, more diverse, flora and fauna than their non-organic counterparts. Look after your allotment and its surroundings organically and you will be helping with conservation too.

Another major shift has been in the attitude to amateur food growing. Over the second half of the 20th century, interest declined and allotments – once vital food sources for the landless town's people – fell into disuse. Lack of interest allowed hundreds of allotment sites to be sold for development. But the tide has now turned, and there are waiting lists for allotments again! Now it is the home garden that is under attack by developers, and Garden Organic has turned its attention to campaigning to prevent this continued loss of amateur growing space.

Women and families are leading the allotment growing revival, taking over what was once a primarily male occupation. These newcomers to growing tend to want to grow organically, using methods that produce healthy crops, without risk to themselves and their children. Adults enjoy having control over how their food is produced and children begin to learn how food can be grown.

There are many good things about allotmenting – exercise, companionship, fresh air and so on – but the prime one, for most people, is of course food growing, and eating! If you have never tasted fresh, organically-grown produce, picked just when it is at its best, you are in for a real treat with your first harvest. There is nothing to beat it for quality and flavour.

An added satisfaction is eating what is available, rather than having to decide what to buy from the shops. Seasonal eating on a plate, with 'food miles' cut to a minimum. Just thinking about those ultra fresh vegetables and fruits makes my mouth water.

This book is based on the sound knowledge and practical experience of the author, Ian Spence, with additional organic input from Garden Organic, the UK's leading organic organization. It will provide you with all the information you need to start an organic allotment, or convert your existing plot to organic management.

Pauline Pears
GARDEN ORGANIC

introduction

For many years organic gardening was thought of as a bit weird and the preserve of sandal-wearing hippy types, but all that has changed. We are now all concerned with what goes into the production of our food and the effect we are having on the environment. Increasingly, we want to take back some control over the food we eat by growing our own, whether that is in our garden or on an allotment. As more people live in flats or in new houses with small gardens, there has been a resurgence in allotment gardening, and this has gone hand in hand with a recognition of the importance of organic methods of production.

The large-scale use of pesticides and artificial fertilizers by farmers is also of increasing concern, while non-organic farmers growing crops on a large scale use these materials to get the required crops, but on an allotment we don't need to use them. For example, a 20 hectare (50 acre) field of cabbages is a magnet for cabbage white butterflies – it's like handing them a meal on a plate, absolute caterpillar heaven – on an allotment we can mix crops together so they don't become such a large target for pests. Many pests find their host plants by sight, so the more we can mix crops together the less chance they will be attacked.

Gardening organically on your allotment is an environmentally friendly way of producing your own food, and it can be done by anyone. It is no harder than any other way of producing food, but the rewards are much greater because we know that the crops have not been sprayed with chemicals, so there is no danger to our families, and the food tastes better.

In the last few years there has been a tremendous uplift in the organic movement, with organic gardening now seen as mainstream. Many governments are now supporting organic farming and gardening with more research, and shops are stocking more organic produce. However, organic crops sold in supermarkets are generally more expensive than their traditionally produced equivalents and many have been flown in from around the world, ironically adding to global pollution. How much better it is to grow your own food on an allotment. Apart from saving money, there is the satisfaction you will gain from growing your own food. The outdoor activity on you allotment will also help to keep you fit and healthy – again, far less expensive than all those visits to a gym.

In addition to the benefits to your health and advantages to your pocket, you will find that many allotment sites are communities in their own right. You will meet like-minded people, all eager to pass on their knowledge gained over many years. Some sites even have their own local produce shows where allotment-holders compete against each other. The prizes aren't great, but the coming together of people from all walks of life forges a real sense of community, something that is sadly lacking in society as a whole. You rarely get that feeling of friendly rivalry and neighbourliness anywhere else other than on an allotment.

Ian Spence

beginning and preparing

Before you start working on your allotment there are a few things to consider that will help ensure success later on. Although they may seem obvious, thinking through what you want to achieve on your allotment and how much time you can devote to it will allow you to make the right choices from the start.

Before you can do anything, you need to get hold of a basic selection of tools – the right choice at this stage will help you work more efficiently and effectively. Then you need to assess what type of soil your allotment has, because this will determine how and when you cultivate it. Clearing the ground, if you have an overgrown plot, will be your first major job, but this can be tackled in stages if the task seems daunting to do all at once.

Practical considerations include identifying a source of water and where to locate your compost heap. Next you need to draw a detailed plan of your plot to establish exactly what goes where. This chapter also explores how to get the most out of your plot, how to rotate your crops and how to make it truly organic, before going into the detail of improving the soil, preparing to plant and learning how to dig, make deep beds, paths, fencing, a compost heap and, finally, a pond.

Making your allotment organic

There is no doubt that making your plot organic will give you tremendous satisfaction. Gardening organically is a better, more sustainable way to produce vegetables and fruit, and your crops will taste better. Your plot may not have been treated organically in the past, but if you start using the methods described in this book it is surprising how quickly the soil and growth of crops will improve. If the soil has not been well cared for it will take a few years to build up the fertility, but the benefits to be gained are worth waiting for. And when things begin to improve you will attract in beneficial wildlife.

Is it organic?

Some organic gardening products, such as fertilizers, composts, seeds and vegetable transplants are available with a recognized organic symbol, which makes choosing them easy. However, not all suitable products have an organic symbol, so you will have to check if these have come from a recognized organic source. It is also important to think about how you can reduce your impact on the environment when choosing products for your plot – recycle, reuse and buy local are the key factors to take into account.

Soil improvers

Using bulky organic matter, such as strawy manure, compost and leaf mould, is the key to a healthy soil. Feed the microorganisms, which keep the soil healthy, and they will convert the organic matter into food the plants can take up. The aim is to build up reserves of organic matter and encourage more microorganisms in

Above Growing your crops organically will result in mouth-watering vegetables and fruits like these apricots.

Right Well-rotted, strawy manure is one of the best soil conditioners. It can be applied as a mulch or dug into the soil.

Clearing the ground

The task of clearing an overgrown allotment may seem daunting, but there are ways of making things easier. First of all, remember that you don't have to clear the entire plot in one go, which would be both difficult and dispiriting. You can cover the rest of the allotment with black polythene. This will prevent weed growth and start killing the weeds until you have time to deal with them. If necessary, use two layers of black polythene to make sure you exclude all light.

If weeds are overgrown and stand several feet tall you will need to cut them down. Do this with a strimmer, a powerful rotary mower or a sythe. Compost all the topgrowth, unless it is woody or is diseased. Once the weed's topgrowth is cut down part of the area can be covered with sheets of cardboard held in place with straw, or another similar material. Alternatively, cover the area with black polythene, anchoring the edges in the soil to hold it in place. This will help prevent regrowth of the weeds until you have time to cultivate a larger area of the plot.

If you want to start using part of your allotment quickly, clear it by digging out the weed roots by hand. Make sure you remove all the roots of perennial weeds as even the smallest piece can regrow. Cover the rest of the allotment with black polythene. Mulching with a sheet mulch will also kill off weeds without digging, but you will have to add a deep layer of 15–20 cm (6–8 in) for it to be effective (see Crop as you clear, page 36). It may take a couple of seasons to get rid of all perennial weeds, but it is worth doing properly, otherwise they remain a problem for years afterwards.

Annual weeds are much easier to clear because you can dig them out, but they may have seeded over the years. Push a hoe through the soil at least once a week, and over a couple of years annual weeds will become less of a problem.

Perennial weeds may also have got in among old fruit trees and soft fruits, such as redcurrants, blackcurrants and gooseberries. Carefully dig out the weeds, making sure that you do not damage the roots of the fruit bushes, which are fairly shallow-rooting plants. It may take a couple of seasons to get rid of the worst perennial weeds, because their roots will be entwined with the roots of the fruit bushes. Persistence will pay off in the end.

the soil over the long-term. Make your own compost on the allotment (see pages 32–3) and bring in organic materials, such as manures, from local sources (see pages 28–30). If all allotment holders get together to buy in bulk the cost will be considerably reduced. It can be difficult to get manures from organic farms, but try to avoid farms that use intensive methods of rearing livestock. Always apply materials in the correct quantities: too much is wasteful and can cause pollution in watercourses. When applied at the correct rate it is surprising how quickly poor soils begin to improve with the addition of organic matter or green manures.

Recycling and composting

Although it's nice to have a bonfire it is best to recycle waste materials in a more sustainable way. A compost heap will take most waste plant material from your allotment (see pages 32–3). If you have a lot of perennial weeds, such as dandelions and docks, compost these in a separate heap covered with a sheet of black polythene – they will take longer to rot down than other material. A compost heap will also cope with most diseased material except persistent diseases such as clubroot and whiterot. Take this type of material to your local recycling centre for large-scale composting.

Wood and wood preservatives

If you need to buy wood for whatever purpose try to make sure it comes from sustainable sources. Look for the FSC (Forest Stewardship Council) logo. When using wood for supports or screens look for coppiced wood such as willow and hazel. Avoid using wood preservatives and source eco-friendly products based on natural plant oils, resins and less toxic materials.

Organic seeds and plants

You can buy organically-grown seeds and plants and these should be your first choice as an organic gardener. However, if you can't find everything you want as organic, you still can buy seeds and plants from a garden centre or nursery even if not organically grown. What we want to do is encourage you to be as organic as you can. Growing your own young plants from seeds and harvesting seeds from crops on your allotment will ensure you only use organically produced materials.

Growing media

If you are raising your own plants to grow on your allotment use an organic seed or multipurpose compost. It should be peat-free and ideally made from recycled materials, from your home country is preferable. There are many different organic growing media available, so it is a question of trying different kinds and finding the one that suits you best.

Organic fertilizers

You may have to use organic fertilizers to begin with until you build up the fertility of the soil with organic matter, such as manure and compost. However, in the longer term it should not be necessary to use any fertilizers other than organic matter (see pages 28–30), unless there is a shortage of organic matter on your allotment when it would be permissible to use some organic fertilizers. Organic fertilizers derive from plant, animal or mineral origin and are slow-acting, releasing their nutrients over a long period (see pages 52–3).

Animal-free products

If you are totally vegetarian and don't like using animal derived fertilizers or soil improvers there are plenty that are animal-free. If this is your preferred way, green manures should be the mainstay of your soil improvement regime.

Resistant cultivars

With experience and talking to fellow allotment holders you will discover which cultivars grow best in your locality. If a particular pest or disease builds to unacceptable levels try to find cultivars that have some resistant to it. When considering planting fruit trees, which are a long-term investment, ask other allotment holders what are the most common problems and look out for resistant cultivars.

Right Seeds such as these dried peas can be saved from plants, and is a way to ensure your seeds are wholly organic. Store them in a cool, dry place.

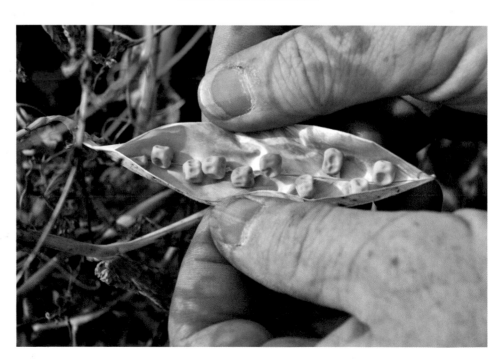

Left Pull up or dig out weeds, as they take moisture and nutrients from the soil and can harbour pests and diseases.

Green manures

Green manures are vigorous crops that are used to protect and improve the soil. They are a valuable tool on an allotment and should be planned into your cropping plan (see page 31).

Weed control

There is no need to reach for a bottle of weedkiller if your plot is very weedy. Use non-chemical methods, such as mulching and digging, to clear weeds and subsequently keep the plot clean. However, weeds do provide food and some shelter for wildlife, so don't worry too much about a few weeds here and there. Only control them where they are interfering with a particular crop. Weeds can be added to the compost heap (see pages 13 and 33).

Pesticides

The aim of organic methods is to grow crops without the need to resort to an arsenal of chemicals to control pests and diseases. However, if a particular problem escalates there are some organic products that can be used. Products containing soft soaps and plant fatty acids are all acceptable organic materials, but as with all pest control methods, use the them according to the manufacturers' instructions. Ask an organic organization for help.

Beneficial wildlife

Beetles
Many species predate on insects as adults and larvae; encourage by disturbing the soil as little as possible and by using mulches.

Centipedes
Eat slugs, slug eggs and other soil-borne pests.

Frogs & toads
Adults feed on a wide variety of pests, especially slugs; encourage them by having a pond.

Hoverflies
The larvae eat aphids; encourage adults by growing single, open-centred flowers.

Lacewings
The larvae eat aphids and similar insects.

Ladybirds
Both adults and larvae eat aphids.

Nematodes
Control slugs and vine weevils.

Spiders
All species predate on insects and not all use webs as traps.

Parasitic wasps
Adult females lay eggs in other insects and the larvae develop inside them, killing them.

Your allotment toolkit

When you buy tools try to get the best quality you can afford. There is little point buying cheap tools – they will not last for long and will make cultivating the soil more difficult. If you can't afford new tools many secondhand tools can be bought at car boot sales and occassionally at flower shows. Whether you buy new or secondhand look after your tools and they will last a life time.

Buy the basics

You don't need to buy the whole shop. A few basic tools will be enough to get you started, and as you progress and try new things you can acquire more as and when you need them. Here is a basic tool kit to get you started. These tools will allow you to tackle most of the jobs that will arise on your organic allotment.

Spade

This is the most-used tool for cultivating soil and planting. If you buy the wrong type it will make cultivation difficult and you may even end up damaging your back. Your spade should suit your size and strength and feel well-balanced when you hold it with one hand at the end of the handle and the other near the top of the blade. D- or T-shaped handles are a matter of personal preference. If you can, buy good-quality stainless steel, which is easy to clean and will last a lifetime without rusting. Forged or hardened steel tools need to be cleaned and rubbed over with an oily rag after use to prevent rusting.

Fork

Use a fork to break down large lumps of soil and for general light cultivation and harvesting vegetables. Choose a good-quality stainless steel or hardened steel fork. It is often easier to dig heavy clay soil with a fork than a spade. Hold it in both hands, like a spade, to make sure it is well balanced and the right size.

Rake

You will need a rake for the final levelling of soil when you are preparing seedbeds. Choose a rake that is forged from a single piece of steel or stainless steel. A long handle will make it easier to use without bending down.

Hoe

Hoes are used to skim off the tops of annual weeds rather than digging up their roots. There is a bewildering range, but all you need to begin with is the traditional Dutch hoe, which is used in a push–pull motion as you walk backwards. Use your hoe when the surface of the soil is dry and it is sunny so the weeds wilt in the sun. Keep the edge sharp to slice through the stems, and get as long a handle as you can so you don't have to stoop.

Garden line

Use a garden line to make straight lines when you are taking out seed drills or planting rows of crops. You don't need anything fancy: two canes and a long piece of string will do perfectly well.

Left A selection of good quality basic gardening tools will make cultivating your allotment a pleasure.

Secateurs

Rake

Spade

Wheelbarrow

Small fork

Trowel

Hoe

Left and above This selection of basic tools will enable you to tackle most jobs on your allotment.

Measuring or planting board

This useful tool enables you to measure the distance between plants. You can make a board from a plank of wood about 1.2 m (4 ft) long. Make saw marks along the plank at 15 cm (6 in) intervals and you will have an easy way of planting out seedlings at the necessary spacing, and use the edge of the board to make short, shallow seed drills across beds.

Watering can

If you have only a few plants a small watering can is perfectly adequate. Over a larger area, however, you will require something more robust. One that holds a maximum of 10 litres (about 2 gallons) is the largest I would recommend. Anything larger is too heavy to carry over any distance. A garden hose is easier, because it cuts down on the endless walking back and forth, but not all allotment sites allow the use of hosepies, and some don't have any water at all.

Secateurs

A good pair of secateurs is essential for pruning. Buy the best you can afford as they will last longer than cheaper models. Hold them in your hand before you buy to make sure they are comfortable. Keep a sharpening stone handy so that the blades always cut cleanly.

Knife

A small, sharp knife can be used in all kinds of ways. Keep the blade sharp and clean.

Trowel

Use a trowel when you are planting smaller plants. You can also use it for light weeding between rows of crops. A good-quality stainless steel one with a well-made wooden handle will last for many years. Some trowels have longer handles, which makes them easier to use and gives greater leverage.

Bucket

A plastic bucket can be used for carrying weeds to your barrow or compost heap and can also double as a watering can.

Wheelbarrow

This tool is indispensable, expecially if you have to cart manure. If there are several allotments on the site you and your fellow holders might consider buying in bulk, and having a wheelbarrow to move your share from a central area will save a lot of legwork. A barrow with a pneumatic tyre is best as it is easier to wheel over rough ground. Don't forget to allow a good width of path to accommodate the barrow, especially when turning it.

Allotment considerations

Before you start work there are a few things to think about. What crops do you want to grow? How much time can you spend? Your main priority should be to grow the crops you like to eat and those that are most expensive to buy. If you stick to this ethos, your efforts will be well rewarded. For example, maincrop potatoes take up a lot of room and are cheap to buy, so you may prefer to use the space for something like succulent garden peas.

Selecting your crops

Growing your own fruit, vegetables and herbs is rewarding, but to get the best from your allotment you should concentrate on growing the crops you eat most often and those that are best eaten fresh from the plot. One consideration to take into account is how expensive crops are to buy in the shops. Choose cultivars that are known for their flavour. It is pointless growing crops with a bland taste – there are plenty of those in the shops. The whole point about growing your own is to harvest produce that is packed with flavour. Ease of growing is, of course, a consideration, especially if you cannot spend much time on the allotment. Some of the easiest crops to grow are listed on page 70. Fruit is a long-term investment, so you should take your time when choosing cultivars and preparing your plot.

Time

The amount of time you can spend on your allotment will depend on your lifestyle and your other commitments. If you are to get the best from the plot you will probably need to tend it for at least one hour every week. Of course, some people almost live on their allotments, installing cooking facilities in the shed and creating a home from home. The more time you spend on your plot, the better your crops will be – for example, you will spot problems, such as pests and diseases, as soon as they arise and will be able to deal with them before they become a major problem.

Right Sinking pots into the soil will get water to where it is most needed, at the plant's roots.

Left Time spent on your allotment will be rewarded with tasty crops through the year, especially during the summer.

Below Growing flowering plants will attract birds to pollinate fruit trees and other beneficial wildlife to control pests.

Water supply

Is there a good water supply on your plot? Increasing concerns about water shortages make a reliable water supply essential, but we still need to conserve as much as possible. It may be that there is only one tap to serve all the allotments, and if a hosepipe ban comes into force, you may spend a lot of time walking back and forth with a watering can. To reduce the amount of watering that is needed use a mulching material to minimize evaporation from the surface of the soil (see pages 54–5).

Shed and greenhouse

If it is permitted, it is a good idea to have a shed, as it will give you somewhere secure to keep your tools so that you do not have to transport them back and forth.

A greenhouse if you have the space and the time – you will need to visit your plot daily – will add immeasurably to the range of crops you can grow. If you have one at home you can raise early crops there before planting them on your allotment.

Being organic

Access to organic matter is the ideal if you want to grow good, healthy crops (see pages 28–30). If you can, buy it in bulk with your fellow allotment holders as it will be more economical. Compost as much waste plant material from your plot as you can. Decaying leaves, fruits and annual weeds can all be added to your heap, and will ultimately improve the fertility of the soil. Woody material, either cut up into small pieces or shredded, can also be added.

Planning your allotment

The plot you take over may have been well looked after, and you may decide you want to retain the existing layout, making changes only when you have worked on it for a while. But even a neat and tidy plot may not be what you need. You may want to make the allotment less labour intensive, for example. If you take over a neglected plot, you have an opportunity to start all over again and develop your allotment exactly the way you want it.

Draw up a plan

Measure your plot and draw a detailed scale plan. Put on everything that is already there – weedy patches, shed, water points, paths and trees – and list all the crops you want to grow and any other features, such as flowerbeds or a pond, that you would like to include. The layout example illustrated here is for a plot measuring 9 x 30 m (30 x 100 ft).

Rotate your crops

Crop rotation is a system by which vegetable crops are grown on different areas of the allotment in succession in consecutive years (see pages 24–5). The main reason for rotating crops is to reduce the incidence of soil-borne pests and diseases specific to each family of crops (see page 70). If the same type of crop is grown in the same area for several years, its pest and disease levels build rapidly often becoming a serious problem.

planting key

1. Grapes on fence
2. Gooseberry and blackcurrant bushes
3. Tomatoes
4. Potatoes
5. Corn
6. Squash
7. Peas and climbing beans
8. Broad beans
9. Leeks
10. Onions
11. Onions and garlic
12. Cabbages, sprouting broccoli and Brussels sprouts
13. Perennial bed – asparagus
14. Carrots and lettuce
15. Beetroot, spinach beets and chard
16. Parsnips
17. Summer raspberries
18. Autumn raspberries

leaf mould Autumn leaves can be stored in a simple wire cage made from chicken wire and four posts, as they do not need heat like a compost heap. Leaves are broken down by fungi. Postion the cage wherever is most convenient.

cut flowers Flowers look good and will attract beneficial insects.

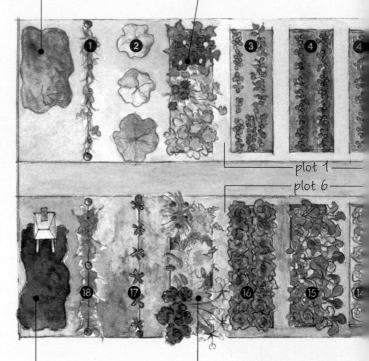

plot 1

plot 6

organic matter storage Position this near the entrance so deliveries of manure can be made conveniently. Stack it under a plastic sheet to rot for three to six months before use, and keep your wheelbarrow handy to transport the manure to where it's needed.

perennial herbs Plants such as fennel, thyme, marjoram, rosemary and chives should be grown in their own bed, but other herbs can be included in the vegetable beds.

compost bins Position
these wherever is most
convenient – halfway
down the allotment is a
good place as it provides
easy access to all areas
of your plot.

pond By by attracting
birds and other creatures
to the allotment a pond
will help create a balanced
environment. Choose a
sunny spot, away from
trees, and install secure
fencing for safety.

a grassy area Somewhere
to rest and recuperate will
be welcome after a hard
day. Tall plants, such as
sunflowers, marigolds
and fennel, against the
boundary fence will give
shade and privacy.

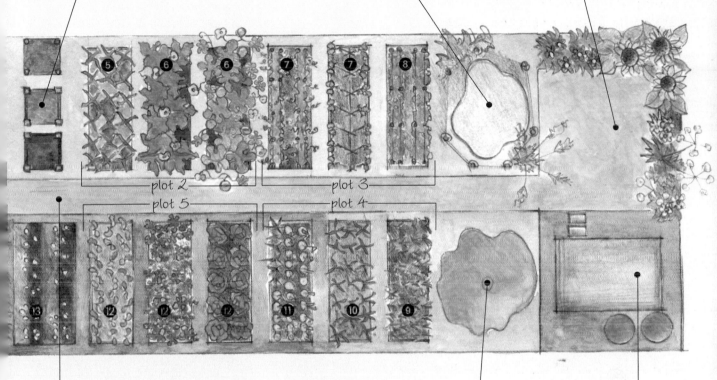

paths and raised beds Separate
crops and areas of intensive cultivation.
To avoid compacting the soil, you
should do all your digging, weeding
and planting from the paths, which
should be at least 60 cm (24 in) wide
to accommodate a wheelbarrow. High
crop returns make up for the space
you have to sacrifice to create them,
however, you might like to grow in
conventional rows across the plot.

fruit tree A fruit tree is a welcome
addition to your allotment. A self-fertile
cultivar is ideal, as it doesn't need a
different cultivar growing nearby to cross
pollinate. However, your tree crop will
be more reliable if there is one growing
nearby, perhaps trained as a cordon (see
page 63).

shed A simple shed
will keep your tools
secure and tidy. Self-
assembly models are
good value, or you
could buy a second-
hand one.

Getting the most from your plot

Once you have made the commitment to having an allotment, it is important to make the most of it. This involves planning your crops so that you have a succession of plants ready to harvest over a long period and so all areas of the plot are used for as much of the year as possible. Ground that lies fallow will only encourage weeds. Keeping good records of what you have grown, where and when, will help you to make the best use of manures and compost, and will make planning of future crops much easier.

Maximizing the space

To get the best use from your allotment maximize all available space. Clear away old crops as you harvest them, and plan ahead so that as soon as one crop has finished you have new seedlings to plant out or seeds to sow in its place to avoid having gaps on the plot. If soil would otherwise be left bare between removing one crop and sowing or planting the next, sow green manures (see page 31). These will help build soil fertility and improve the soil structure.

Make use of the space between rows. Brussels sprouts, for example, take up a lot of room, but the ground between the rows can be used for smaller, fast-growing crops, such as lettuce. This is known as intercropping. You can also grow lettuce and other salad crops on ridges between rows of plants, such as blanching celery. This is known as catch cropping. Using the bed system maximizes the number of vegetables you can grow in the space. These beds, which are just 1.2 m (4 ft) wide, will enable you to grow crops close together (see page 34).

Another way to use every inch of space is to grow tender crops, such as melons, cucumbers and tomatoes, on top of a compost heap that has been built up to its maximum size then left to decompose. Put a layer of soil on top of the heap and plant directly into this.

Above Use the space between sweetcorn to grow squashes or pumpkins.

Avoiding gluts

Most vegetable seeds are sown in spring, and many gardeners end up with a glut of crops to harvest in late summer and early autumn. Don't feel that you have to sow an entire packet of seeds all at once. Spreading the sowing over two or three weeks will mean that the crops don't mature at the same time.

Thinning out and transplanting will also, in a small way, help to avoid gluts. As seedlings are transplanted from the row where they were sown, the roots of the seedlings are damaged to some degree. This means the transplanted seedlings will mature slightly more slowly than those left in the row undisturbed.

Extending the season

Choose types of plants that are appropriate for each season. It may seem obvious, but spring cabbage gives a good spring harvest, summer cabbage is ready for summer harvesting, and winter cabbage will be ready for picking in winter.

Using your greenhouse if you have one, or cold frames and cloches will allow you to start crops earlier in the year and will protect them as autumn days turn cooler. You can also use horticultural fleece and fine mesh netting to protect crops from frost.

Sowing winter salads, such as lettuce, corn salad and rocket, in late summer and autumn will also extend the season. In colder areas or severe winter weather these may need the protection of cloches or cold frames.

Autumn onions are also a good crop to sow to extend the growing season. The seeds of these are sown in autumn (or you can buy autumn onion sets) and are harvested in early summer the following year. Garlic is another crop that can be planted in autumn as well as spring to extend the season.

Below When using netting to protect crops from birds make sure the netting is secure so they don't get tangled in it.

Right Annual weeds and green manures can be dug in to return nutrients to the soil for the next crop.

Left If you cannot afford a ready-made greenhouse, a simple structure made from wood and polythene is the next best thing.

Rotating your crops

Crop rotation means growing crops that belong to the same family group in different areas each year. There are several reasons for doing this: pests and diseases, soil additives, soil structure, nutrition and controlling weeds. Permanent crops, such as asparagus and rhubarb, need a separate area to themselves, outside the normal crop rotation area. Don't forget fruit. Tree fruits, such as apples and pears, need a permanent spot, although they can be grown within beds, but strawberries can be included within a normal crop rotation plan because they are not a permanent crop and need to be replaced every few years.

Crop rotation plan — year one

Plot a	Plot b	Plot c	Plot d

Plot a

Family
Solanaceae, Cucurbitaceae

Required Treatment
In spring dig in the green manure grazing rye (see plot D) and apply organic matter. After harvesting early potatoes, plant *Alliaceae* (see plot B) to grow over winter – they need no additional feeding.

Crops
- aubergines
- cucumbers
- marrows
- melons
- peppers
- potatoes
- pumpkins
- tomatoes

Plot b

Family
Papillionacea, Alliaceae

Required Treatment
Plants will benefit from a leaf mould mulch. Follow with a late summer sowing of the green manure winter tares to fix nitrogen for next year's brassicas. On poorer soils onions and leeks might require compost.

Crops
- beans
- garlic
- leeks
- onions
- peas

Plot c

Family
Brassicaceae, Poaceae

Required Treatment
Dig in winter tares or add compost in spring; mulch with leaf mould in autumn.

Crops
- Brussels sprouts
- broccoli
- cabbages
- calabrese
- cauliflowers
- Chinese cabbage
- kale
- kohl rabi
- sweetcorn
- radishes
- rocket
- swedes
- turnips

Plot d

Family
Chenopodiaceae, Apiaceae

Required Treatment
These are mostly root crops, which don't require extra feeding. In spring apply compost where celery and leaf beet are to grow. Follow with the green manure grazing rye to cover the soil in winter.

Crops
- chard
- beetroot
- carrots
- celery
- celeriac
- parsnips
- Hamburg parsley
- spinach beet

Left Looking after your soil means
you can grow crops like this
succulent sweetcorn.

Weed control Controlling weeds is desirable. Crops such as potatoes and marrows, which produce masses of foliage, are good at suppressing weeds because the leaves reduce light at soil level. Onions and carrots, on the other hand, are not so good for weed control, so alternating these crops will help keep weeds at bay.

Liming Lime is added to the *Brassicaceae* family section of your plot in autumn, when the soil's pH level (see page 27) may need to be raised to control clubroot. Use ground limestone or dolomitic limestone. Don't apply it where you are growing potatoes, as this encourages scab.

Reasons for crop rotation

Rotating crops is an important part of allotment management, reducing attacks from pests and diseases and enabling you to make the best use of organic matter and fertilizers applied to the soil.

Pests and diseases Vegetables from the same family tend to be attacked by the same pests and diseases. For example, potato eelworm, clubroot of cabbages and cauliflowers (and all other brassicas) and onion white rot all survive in the soil for many years. Moving potential host plants from the soil and planting something from a group that is not susceptible to the pest will keep infestation down.

Nutrition All vegetables have different nutrient requirements, and moving them around the allotment prevents the depletion, or build-up, of particular nutrients from and in the soil.

Soil additives Some crops need additional fertilizers to do well, but others can make use of nutrients left behind by crops from the year before. Types of beans and peas, for example, fix nitrogen in the soil, so you could grow sweetcorn, which does well in nitrogen-rich soils, in the part of the plot used to grow beans the previous year. The roots of some plants, such as carrots, tend to fork in freshly manured soil, so grow these on land manured the previous year. Grow plants with similar requirements together so that you can conveniently add appropriate fertilizers and other treatments, if they are necessary.

Crop rotation plan

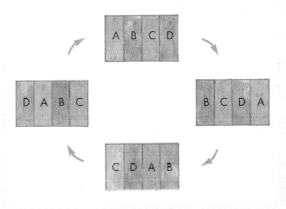

A crop rotation plan should last for a minimum of four years, but preferably for six or more, and some plans are worked out over 12 years. The cycle of pests and diseases can be effectively disrupted in an organic allotment only if you remove potential hosts until the pest or pathogen is inactive.

To get you started, illustrated above is a simple four-year plan. You can adapt the plan to suit the particular crops you are growing. Divide your allotment or beds into four areas and identify the crops you want to grow in each area, remembering to keep vegetables of the same family in each group (see page 70).

Types of soil

Soil is the basic raw ingredient needed for plants to grow, so you should treat it with reverence. It contains rock particles that have been broken down over millions of years, but a large part of it is derived from organic matter – the broken-down remains of plants and animals. Air and water are also necessary for plants to grow, and these are present in varying quantities, according to the type of soil you have on your allotment. All these ingredients provide a home for millions of bacteria and other microscopic creatures, which are essential for healthy plant growth and a healthy, productive soil.

Below You can tell the structure of your soil by rubbing a sample between your fingers.

Soil types

There are many different types of soil, ranging from light sandy ones to the heaviest clay that can be very difficult to cultivate, but they can be broadly divided into five main groups: clay, sandy, silt, chalky and peaty.

The type of soil you have will determine when you can cultivate and how best to do so. For example, heavy clay soils are cold and wet and take longer to warm up in spring than sandy soils, so you may have to start sowing in a clay soil several weeks later than in a sandy soil. Of course, you can overcome all these problems by covering the soil with polythene or cloches during the wettest months of winter, and this will allow you to make a start with sowing and planting no matter what the weather, but more of this later (see page 54).

Clay Clay soils are cold and heavy and slow to warm up in spring. They feel sticky when moist but are hard and compacted when dry. The particles of clay soils are very small, making them poorly drained and difficult to work in wet conditions. You can, however, improve this type of soil by adding organic matter, which helps improve the soil structure making it easier to cultivate. Clay soils can be quite productive because they are naturally rich in nutrients and minerals.

Sandy These soils are light and easy to cultivate. The soil feels gritty when you rub it between your fingers because the sand particles are larger than clay soil particles. Sandy soils warm up quickly in spring and are good for early crops, because the soil can be cultivated earlier and in most weather conditions. However, sandy soils are free draining, which means nutrients are easily leached by rains, so they need the addition of plenty of organic matter to improve their fertility and make them more moisture retentive. Keep the soil covered with a mulch or a green manure at all times.

Silt Silt soils fit somewhere between clay and sand – they are neither too gritty nor too sticky. When you rub particles between your fingers they feel smooth and silky. However, when very wet silt tends to compact, making it badly drained. It is possible to improve the texture of silt soils, opening the soil up, by adding organic matter, compost or manure in autumn or spring.

Chalk Chalky soils are usually thin and 'hungry'. They often contain a lot of stones and flints, and they are very free draining. The topsoil is usually shallow, which makes it difficult for plant roots to penetrate deep into the soil, so they lose water and nutrients easily. Chalk soils are very alkaline (containing a lot of lime), making them inhospitable to many plants.

Peat These soils, which tend to look dark, almost black, are rich in organic matter. They are usually easy to dig but are often acidic (with a pH below 6.0), so are not suitable for all crops. Add lime to raise the pH to 7.0 or higher. They sometimes also dry out completely in dry, hot summers and can be difficult to re-wet.

Soil pH

Soil pH is a measurement of the acidity or alkalinity of the soil. The pH scale is numbered from 1 (extremely acid) to 14 (extremely alkaline) with 7 being neutral. The majority of vegetables prefer growing in the range 6.5–7 and fruit 6–6.5.

The pH of the soil governs the availability of nutrients. In very acid soils nutrients can be washed out or be at toxic levels to the plants in the soil. However, in alkaline soils nutrients can be locked up in the soil making them unavailable to plants. Soil pH can also have an effect on some diseases in the soil. For instance, potato scab is more prevalent on alkaline soils while clubroot of brassicas is much less of a problem. In acid soils wireworms can be troublesome.

Testing your soil pH An initial test of the soil on your allotment is a good idea. This will let you know how acid or alkaline the soil is. Easy-to-use soil testing kits are available from garden centres. You will need to take samples from various parts of the allotment to get an overall reading.

You can also buy inexpensive meters that have a probe that is inserted into the soil and displays a reading. It's perhaps not the most accurate way, but does give you a rough guide.

Changing the soil pH

If the soil is too alkaline, which can be a common problem on allotments where the soil has been limed too often, there is little you can do. Applying sulphur pellets may reduce alkalinity but it is a long process. The pH will gradually become more acid over the years. If it is too acid, then liming may be necessary.

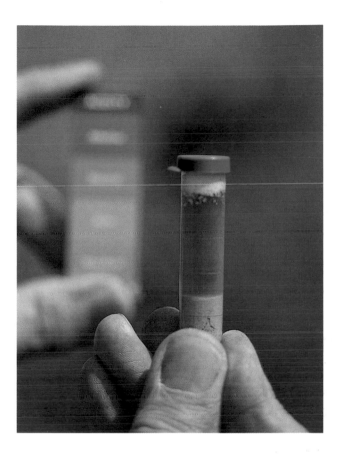

Above Soil pH test kits are available from garden centres and are easy to use. They are not exact but give a general guide to soil pH.

Different types of lime There are two types of lime suitable to use on an organic allotment – dolomitic limestone and ground limestone. Dolomitic limestone (calcium magnesium carbonate) will supply calcium and magnesium; ground limestone (calcium carbonate) will supply calcium. These are slow acting limestones and are usually applied in autumn so they act on the soil before the next growing season. The rate of application will depend on how acid your soil is, but a general rate is 200 g/sq m (7 oz/sq yd) on a soil with an average pH of 5.00–6.00.

Liming Lime is usually only needed where brassicas (cabbage family) are to be grown, and only if the soil is not alkaline enough for them (see above). You should only need to apply lime once every three to four years, so always test your soil first before applying lime. Apply lime on a calm day and wear gloves, goggles and a mask. Wash any exposed skin thoroughly after use.

Improving your soil

Soil is the basis of all gardening and you need to look after it and nurture it to achieve the best possible crops. No soil is perfect, and all soils have advantages and disadvantages, but you have to work with what you've got and improve it as much as you can. The main reason for improving your soil is to encourage an active, diverse range of soil microlife. This is done by adding what are known as bulky organic materials – dead and decaying plant remains or animal manures.

Treating your soil

How you treat your soil will depend on what type it is – light sandy soil, heavy clay soil or something in between. You will also need to consider what was grown in the allotment patch in the past and what you want to grow in the future. Sandy soils are free-draining and lose nutrients in wet weather, while heavy clay soils hold on to water and nutrients. Your soil may be nutrient rich already, so a good idea will be to test it. Soil testing kits can be bought from garden centres.

All types of soils can be improved by incorporating organic matter that is dug into the soil or used as a mulch spread over the soil surface (see page 55). Worms will gradually work it into the lower layers of the soil. Organic matter will open up heavy clay soils improving their structure and making them easier to cultivate. On sandy soils, organic matter will help to bind the soil particles so they hold moisture and nutrients better.

Strawy animal manures are often used to improve soils. Horse and farmyard manure are the most common, and have a medium to high fertility rating. The nutrient content, however, will vary depending on the proportion of manure and urine to straw. Also, if the manure is stored outside nitrogen and potassium are easily leached out with heavy rain. Unless bought already well-rotted you will need to stack the manure for at least 12 months to allow it to rot down well.

Other organic materials to consider are spent mushroom compost that has medium fertility; green waste compost, which has low fertility but is a good source of potassium (see page 30); leaf mould, which is low in fertility but is good used as mulch (see page 30); and spent hops, which are also low in fertility.

For high-fertility soil improvers use up to one barrow load (50 l/11 gal) per 5 m² (6 yd²) making a 5 mm (⅛ in) deep layer. For medium soil improvers use up to two barrow loads (100 l/22 gal) per 5 m² (6 yd²), making a layer about 1 cm (⅜ in) deep. Low-fertility materials can be applied in greater quantities.

Soil improvers

Time spent adding improvers to the soil is never wasted. There are numerous materials to add to soil, however, whatever you choose your aim is to create a fertile, moisture-retentive but free-draining soil.

Check that any improver you buy is from an accredited organic source. That means if you buy manures from stables or a farm that the animals are reared organically – they are fed with natural foods and are not treated with drugs. If in doubt contact an accredited organic association for advice.

Left Organic matter is one of the best soil conditioners to use. Dig it in during autumn or spring.

Applying organic matter to soil

The exact nutrient levels of the organic matter you use will vary depending on the type and age of the material, where it has been stored, and what has been put on the compost heap. However, below is a rough guide.

High nutrient levels
Well-rotted manure stored under cover.

Medium nutrient levels
Garden compost and manure not stored under cover.

Low nutrient levels (slow release)
Leaf mould and green waste compost.

High- and medium-nutrient organic matter should be applied in the spring and summer only. Use no more than one to two wheelbarrow loads per 10 m² (12 yd²) of ground. Low-nutrient organic matter can be applied at any time of the year.

Apply bulky organic matter to the soil surface as a mulch or fork it into the top 20 cm (8 in) of the soil, where the bulk of the biological activity takes place.

Organic matter The more organic material (the dead and decomposing remains of living things, for example plant and animal manures) you dig in the better, and well rotted farmyard manure is best of all. Apply horse manure at the rate of one barrow to 5 m² (6 yd²) of soil and slightly more for compost from the compost bin. Horse manure is slightly better for clay soils because it tends to be slightly warmer than farmyard manure. Only use well-rotted manure. If it is not well rotted it will scorch or burn the roots of plants.

As soil microorganisms feed on the organic matter, their activities help to create a good soil structure – one that holds water but does not become waterlogged. The microbes also make any plant foods in the organic matter available to the plant roots. Don't use too much nutrient-rich organic matter as overfeeding can make plants more attractive to pests, and nutrients from it can be leached into the environment.

Seaweed If you live near to a beach, seaweed is an excellent soil conditioner. It helps to bind soil particles together, thus improving the structure of the soil, and it is particularly rich in trace elements, which plants need in small quantities. You will need to check if you need to get permission before collecting seaweed from a beach.

Spent mushroom compost The mixture of horse manure, peat and chalk used by commercial mushroom growers is a useful soil conditioner, but it is slightly alkaline. This shouldn't be a problem on an allotment, but you should check your soil for acidity or alkalinity with a testing kit before applying it. Some mushroom growers treat their compost with pesticides, so only buy compost from an accredited organic mushroom grower.

Spent hops If you're lucky enough to have a brewery nearby try spent hops, which are a by-product of the

Right Organic fertilizers are materials of plant, mineral or animal origin that break down slowly when added to the soil. They include materials such as rock phosphate, bonemeal and wood ash. Bulky organic manures and composts should be the main source of plant foods on an organic allotment, but organic fertilizers can be a useful supplement at times.

brewing industry and are a good soil conditioner. They will add a small amount of nutrients as well.

Green waste compost This is the term usually used for compost produced on a large scale from parks, and garden waste taken to recycling centres and waste disposal sites. It may be available from your local recycling centre or ask your local council. Green waste compost is a type of organic matter and is a good source of potassium. It also contains nitrogen, but this is released very slowly.

Garden compost A compost heap is the heart of every allotment, and every gardener should have one. The ideal materials to use on a compost heap consist of a 50:50 mix by volume of green and brown vegetation – some tough material that is woody is also helpful in maintaining the structure of the heap. To rot down properly compost needs air as well as moisture. There is no need to turn a compost heap, but turning it two or three times will benefit the breaking down of the material in the heap. To turn your compost move partially rotted material toward the centre of the heap. A good compost will be sweet smelling and crumbly (see pages 32–3).

Making leaf mould

Leaf mould is easy to make from leaves that have fallen from deciduous trees in the autumn. If there aren't many trees on the allotment site your local authority may deliver leaves that they have collected from around the area. Ask for leaves from parks and cemeteries, rather than street swept leaves.

The simplest way to make leaf mould is to stack the leaves in a tidy heap or, if there aren't many leaves to collect, put them in a black polythene bag with a few holes punched into the bag to allow some air in. Leave the heap or the bag of leaves for up to two years.

Alternatively, the leaves can be contained by knocking four wooden posts into the soil and attaching chicken wire netting to these to form a container. The size of the container will depend on the amount of leaves you have. Place the leaves in the container, soaking any that are dry with some water, and leave them to rot down for a year or two before use.

Green manures

A very easy and successful way to improve the quality of the soil organically is to use green manures. These are plants that are specifically grown as crops to benefit the soil by improving soil fertility and structure, drainage and waterholding, and weed control.

Growing green manures

A range of plants can be used as green manures, and those in the *Leguminosae* family take up (fix) nitrogen from the air increasing soil fertility. Green manure crops will take up and hold on to soil nutrients preventing them from being washed down through the soil. Once dug in and decomposed the nutrients in green manures are returned to the soil to be taken up by the next crop sown. Green manures also provide a protective layer over the soil protecting it from heavy rain, which destroys soil structure, especially in winter.

You can sow green manures anytime of the year from the spring through to the autumn. Prepare the soil as you would for other seeds, rake it so the ground is level, then scatter (broadcast) the seeds or sow them in drills (see page 46).

Green manures should be dug back into the ground before the plants get too tough. For annual green manures this means before they flower. This can be a few weeks to a few months after sowing, depending on the time of year and type of plant. Longer-term types, such as clover, can be cut down when they flower – the regrowth will be young and tender. Allow three to four weeks for the green manure to decompose before sowing or planting.

When the time comes to dig in the green manure plants use a spade to turn the plants back into the soil, chopping up any clumps thoroughly as you go. If you are using the no dig system (see page 36), cover the plants with a mulch to kill off the top growth (see pages 54–5).

Selection of green manures

Field beans

FAMILY: *Leguminosae*
SOW: Autumn
DIG IN: Spring
BEST FOR: Fixing nitrogen into the soil

Tares, winter

FAMILY: *Leguminosae*
SOW: Spring to autumn or to overwinter
DIG IN: 2 or 3 months after sown
BEST FOR: Weed suppressor

Rye, Hungarian grazing

FAMILY: *Gramineae*
SOW: Autumn
DIG IN: Spring
BEST FOR: Improving both sandy and clay soils

Phacelia

FAMILY: *Hydrophyllaceae*
SOW: Spring to autumn
DIG IN: 1 to 2 months after sown
BEST FOR: Attracting bees

Creating your compost heap

The compost heap is an absolutely essential part of every allotment. You can put all your weeds and vegetable waste from your allotment and from the kitchen on to the heap, and it will eventually turn into wonderful, friable organic matter. It is the best recycling method there is.

Above Two compost bins are ideal. While one heap is rotting down the other bin can be filled with new materials.

How to get good compost

A compost heap is essential for every allotment and the best compost is made from a wide range of materials all mixed together. It is a great facility for recycling waste that produces a first class soil improver.

Making compost is easy and anyone can do it – the process of converting waste products to compost is carried out by various microbes and creatures in the soil. You can make a simple covered heap directly on the ground or use some sort of compost container.

Plant waste

The most obvious way to recycle all plant waste from the allotment is by composting it. Ideally, have more than one compost bin, because you will collect more waste than you realize. If you add food waste from home, the only items you should not to put on the heap are cooked food and bones, which will attract vermin.

The main ingredients of the heap are likely to be a mix of 'greens' and 'browns' – greens are sappy materials, such as grass mowings, and browns are all the tougher materials, such as old vegetable plants. Use a good mixture of the materials and make sure any dry material is dampened with water before putting it on the heap.

Most diseased material can be put on a compost heap with the exception of material affected by very persistent diseases, such as clubroot of brassicas, and white rot of onions, which is very difficult to eradicate so ask your local authority where is the best place to dispose of affected plants. Chop up thick stems of brassicas so they rot down more quickly.

Add material to the heap as it becomes available and mix it up occasionally. It may be difficult to fill a container all at once, in which case it will take the material some considerable time to rot down, perhaps upto a year. However, if you can fill it in one go the material will heat up and rot down more quickly. At the end of a year or more you should have friable, sweet-smelling compost to use as a mulch (see pages 54–5) or to dig in (see pages 34–5).

Compost containers

You can use almost any material to make a compost container. The main points to consider are that the sides must help to retain heat, they must be strong enough to hold a lot of material, they must allow you to reach the composted material easily and, finally, they must look reasonably good.

Wood The container can have slatted timber sides, but solid timber sides will retain more heat, speeding up the decomposing process. Old pallets are useful, but they do have a lot of gaps. However, you can line the sides with cardboard to increase insulation. And once the cardboard has rotted you can dig it in to the soil with the compost or put it on the next heap.

Only use wood, slatted or solid, that has come from a sustainable source – look for the FSC (Forest Stewardship Council) logo.

Plastic There is a range of styles and sizes of plastic container, and some are made of recycled plastic. Most are simple inverted cones that sit on the ground, and when you want to get to the compost you have to lift up the bin. Some models have 'doors' near the base so that you can get to the compost more easily. Some green-minded local authorities provide them at a reduced price to encourage compost-making.

Chicken wire For the simplist and most cost efficient container all you need is chicken wire and four posts.

You will have to line it with cardboard to retain some heat, but it is highly effective. Make it whatever size is convenient, but the larger the better.

Composting weeds

Weeds are a valuable addition to the compost heap. The soil attached to the roots of weeds increases the amount of organisms in the compost, which help to break down materials in the heap. Annual weeds such as groundsel, annual meadow grass and common chickweed are fine to use. These plants germinate, grow, flower, set seeds and die in one year, so there is no problem with them regrowing unless they are seeding when you put them on your heap. Mixed with other materials, annual weeds soon rot down to be returned to the soil.

Making a compost heap

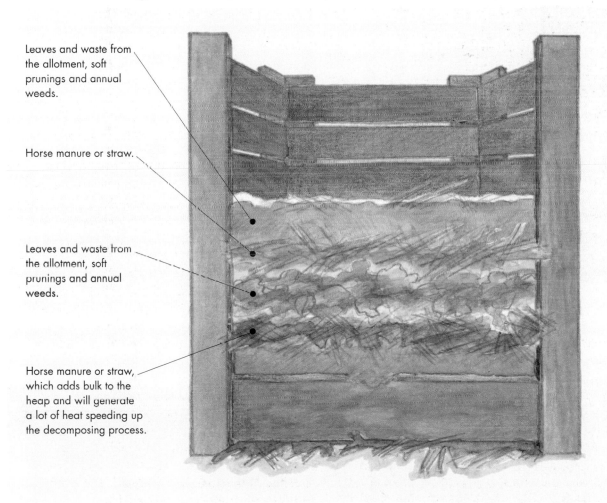

Leaves and waste from the allotment, soft prunings and annual weeds.

Horse manure or straw.

Leaves and waste from the allotment, soft prunings and annual weeds.

Horse manure or straw, which adds bulk to the heap and will generate a lot of heat speeding up the decomposing process.

Soil preparation

Soil is key to how successfully your plants will grow, so looking after a healthy and fertile soil should be your priority. No soil is perfect, however, and all types are capable of being improved. Your main task when looking after the soil should be maintaining a good soil structure, which is the way it is put together. For example, heavy clay soils can be difficult to work, but are rich in plant foods, whereas light sandy soils are easy to work, but nutrients are leached out by rain. There are several ways of cultivating your soil – traditional digging, the no-dig approach and something in between, such as the bed system. The method you choose will depend on how you want to grow your crops and the amount of time and effort you want to put into your allotment.

Digging

On a traditional allotment long rows of vegetables are usually grown across the plot. This is a perfectly good way of growing vegetables – it allows a large area to be cultivated and the space can be used with great flexibility. And long, straight rows of crops look great.

Growing vegetables, however, require attention such as watering, weeding, sowing, thinning and harvesting. To perform these tasks you have to tread over the soil, which in turn becomes compacted. The air in the soil is reduced, impeding drainage and resulting in poor growth. You can minimize compaction by avoiding walking on the soil when it is very wet or by laying down planks to walk on to spread your weight as you work, but you will still need to dig your plot each year.

The main reasons for digging other than to break up compacted soil, are to remove weeds and to add soil improvers. Also, while you are digging some soil-borne pests will be brought to the surface to be eaten by birds – and the company of birds when digging is a pleasure.

Digging tips

- Use a well-balanced spade or fork.
- All lighter soils should be dug in spring.
- Dig heavy clay soils in autumn and leave them rough over winter, as winter weather will break down the soil clods. Let Mother Nature do a lot of the work for you.
- Don't dig when the soil is so wet it sticks to your boots.
- Cover an area of the plot with black polythene to keep off the worst rains.

Digging is one of those jobs you either love or hate, however, it can be a pleasant job and is great exercise if done properly. It is best not to tackle too much at one time. Perhaps dig for an hour, then do something else that does not involve bending your back for a while.

The bed system

The bed system is a way of growing vegetables in narrow beds. The beds can be as long as you like and any shape, just as long as they are no more than 1.2 m (4 ft) wide, so you can easily reach the centre. The advantage of this is that cultivations can be done from the paths on either side of the beds without stepping on the soil – this avoids soil compaction. Also, other tasks like weeding can be done soon after it has rained.

There is another great advantage – once beds are dug over initially they should need little digging again. You can, however, dig them each year if you want (see How to dig, opposite).

Since the soil in a bed system is not compacted crops can be grown more closely than in traditional long rows, increasing the yield from a given area. The bed system also makes planning your plot easier.

Types of beds There are several types of beds variously described as flat or semi-flat, deep or raised beds. Flat or semi-flat beds are easily marked out with string and cultivated, whereas raised beds look better with an edging, such as untreated scaffold planks, or you can use recycled timber. The edging should be around 10–15 cm (4–6 in) wide. Make the southern side of the bed slightly lower (or northern side if you live in the southern hemisphere) and create a shallow slope to help the soil warm up quickly in the spring.

Paths The paths between beds can be compacted soil, but you will have to skim off the weeds when they grow. Alternatively, put down a weed-suppressing landscape fabric (or any old sheets of polythene) and cover it with a mulch of bark chippings or something similar. Make your paths wide enough both to take a wheelbarrow and to turn it easily.

Right With the bed system you can grow crops close together as the soil is not compacted by treading on it.

How to dig

1 Take out a trench halfway across the plot, digging one spade deep and one spade wide. Once the trench is dug move the soil to the other side of the plot – it will be used to fill in the very last trench dug. It can be useful to put a length of string down the middle of the plot so that you work in line.

2 Put compost or manure in the bottom of the trench just dug. Start digging the next trench and throw the soil on to the trench in front, turning it with the compost and manure as you do so. Continue this process until you reach the other end of the plot.

3 Fill in the last trench on this side with soil from the other half of the plot. This automatically takes out your trench to go back along the other side of the plot. Repeat, putting compost in the bottom and covering it with soil as described in step 2. When you reach the end fill in the last trench with the soil you took out in step 1.

No-dig system

This is an organic technique that can be used for growing a wide range of crops. It works on the basis that too much digging can be detrimental to the soil structure, as digging increases the rate organic matter decomposes and results in moisture loss into the air. Once an initial cultivation is done when preparing the plot the soil is never turned over again. Soil improvers are spread over the surface, but not incorporated into the soil – earthworms and other organisms do this job. Some disturbance of the soil is inevitable as you sow and harvest crops, but it will be minimal.

Getting started Initially you may have to dig the soil to relieve compaction and to improve soil structure. If there are no major problems with your soil you can start planting and sowing right away, but before you start apply appropriate soil improvers. If the soil is weedy lay down some sheet mulch (see below).

Sowing or planting The majority of crops are grown in the same way as when using a traditional row or the bed system – seeds are sown in drills and transplants planted in holes. Before planting scrape back the layer of soil improver, then spread it back over the soil when you have finished. If sowing, wait until the plants have germinated before you spread back the soil improver.

Dig or no dig?

The benefits of no-dig

- You don't have to dig the soil.
- Soil structure is preserved and in time improved.
- Earthworms and other soil organisms thrive in undisturbed soil.
- Fewer weed seeds are brought to the surface.

The disadvantages of no-dig

- It can take longer to improve poorer soils.
- Soil-borne pests are not exposed to predators.
- Compacted soil, like heavy soil, still needs cultivating before sowing or planting.

Crop as you clear

Cut down weeds and leave them in situ, then cover the ground with opened out, cardboard cartons, overlapping the edges well – top with 15–20 cm (6–8 in) organic matter, such as leaf mould, grass mowings, spoiled straw and mushroom compost. After a few weeks, seed potatoes and sturdy transplants can be planted through the cardboard. Top up mulch through the season, as necessary. Most weeds will be killed by the end of the season, but some perennials may take longer.

Your allotment shed

An allotment won't be an allotment without a shed, and every plot should have one. Sheds are an important part of the allotment landscape, and they are often made out of any material that comes to hand – the variety of shapes, colours and sizes on an allotment site are a sight to behold. Sheds can provide convenient hiding places for all kinds of creatures – even gardeners can be found lurking in there, drinking tea or just watching the world go by. They are mostly used for storing tools, fertilizers, seats, gas stoves for brewing tea and all those other bits and pieces that accumulate over the years. Some sheds even sport carpets, making them a cosy shelter during bad weather.

Choosing a shed

There are many different types of sheds on the market. The kind you have will depend on what you can afford, and, if your allotment is on a municipal or publicly owned site, the size will depend on what the local authority will permit.

There is no doubt that a shed for storing tools will save you from having to transport your tools to the allotment every time you go. Make sure that your shed is quite sturdy and remember to lock it when you are away from the allotment. Garden tools and other equipment are expensive to buy and are attractive to thieves. Most allotment sites are locked, but it is wise to take additional security measures.

The traditional pitched roof shed is available in many sizes. These sheds are usually made of wood, with a door at one end and windows on one side.

Sheds with a single sloped roof are also widely available. They are also usually made of wood with the door on the front. They are just as useful and hold just as much as sheds with pitched roofs.

Metal sheds are becoming increasingly popular. Their great advantage is that they do not need treating with wood preservative and will last for many years.

Left Allotment sheds are part of the landscape. They are a useful place to store tools and other things you cannot do without.

Making paths

You will need pathways to walk on to reach your crops and to work from. Because they take up space that could be used for crops, it is best to keep paths to a minimum, but ensure they are wide enough to walk on comfortably and to turn a wheelbarrow. If you use the bed system (see pages 34–5) you will need paths around them so that you can reach into the beds; it can seem that the paths take up too much space, but because the crops are close together in deep beds, you actually get a heavier yield than if you grow them in traditional beds. In a standard allotment it is usual to have one path down the centre of the plot. One or two across the width of the plot will also be helpful.

Materials

There is a wide range of materials that you can use for paths, and the one you choose will depend on what you prefer and how deep your pockets are. However, there is no need to go to great expense to make paths – after all, they will not be taking heavy traffic. To prevent weeds from growing through put down a membrane, such as polythene or a geotextile (see page 54), before adding you chosen material.

Chipped bark Although it is more expensive than gravel, chipped bark is good to look at and produces a lovely smell that rises when you step on it. There are various grades and colours, and bear in mind you will have to top it up every year.

Straw Straw can be useful for a temporary path, but it will eventually rot and it can become messy during wet weather. Use it between rows of crops to help suppress weeds. When finished with, add it to your compost heap to rot down or dig in directly to the soil.

Grass A grass path is traditional, but grass needs regular cutting and edging to keep the allotment looking neat and tidy. It will also take nutrients and moisture from the soil. If the path is too narrow it will quickly become messy and worn, particularly during wet spells.

Left Good paths will make working on your allotment much easier. Make sure the paths are reasonably level and firm.

Below Ornamental plants and herbs make an attractive edging breaking up the lines of the path.

Erecting fencing and trellis

You might want to create a secluded corner in your allotment, and the easiest way to achieve this is by using fencing or trellis. There are many products available, including fencing panels, but you can make trellis quite easily from roofing battens, which will be cheaper and more satisfying. Fencing has a secondary value. In addition to providing some privacy, it will create a micro-climate in the immediate area, providing shelter for crops and encouraging them to grow more quickly. Treat the section of the wood that goes into the soil with a preservative that is not harmful to plants and animals – or use wood that will last without treating.

Types of fencing

If an existing fence is old and falling apart it will be worth talking to your neighbouring allotment-holder about replacing it altogether. Your neighbour might be willing to share the cost, and it's worth choosing a style that you both like if it is visible from both plots.

Panel fencing Most garden centres and large DIY stores stock a bewildering array of styles of panel fencing. Choose whichever style takes your fancy, but only use wood from sustainably managed forests. The panels are made from thin wood and will need treating with wood preservative every few years, which will introduce chemicals to your organic allotment. If the panels are erected so that they do not touch the ground, you might find that a water-repellent stain is sufficient. The posts should be securely set in concrete.

Overlap fencing The vertical pieces of timber are nailed to horizontal supports, and each piece of timber overlaps the next one. This type of fencing is similar to panel fencing (see above), and the wood needs the same treatment.

Above Hurdle fencing (back) is expensive, so an inexpensive option is using scraps of wood (front).

Trellis

The great advantage of trellis is that it allows the wind to filter through. It will not give instant privacy, but plants will quickly cover it and give you a secluded spot.

It is fairly easy to make you own trellis from wooden roofing battens. Set posts in the ground at 2 m (6 ft) intervals and make up panels of trellis to fit between each one. You can arrange the battens to make squares, diamonds or rectangles. The posts are best set in concrete to keep them firmly anchored. You can also get special metal post-holders that protect the base of the post from the moisture in the ground.

Your allotment pond

Water is an essential feature in an organic allotment. Even something as simple as putting out a small dish of water for birds to drink from will attract them from all over the area.

If you have space, however, think about having a proper pond. It doesn't have to be big to be effective – even a small pond will encourage wildlife to the allotment, and a half-barrel pond is better than nothing. The pond will be used by many creatures for different purposes. Birds will drink from it and bathe in it, and other creatures will hunt for food in it. If you use a container, sink it in the ground so that it won't heat up too much and if any creatures falls in they can get out again easily. Always check with the allotment rules before embarking on building a pond.

Attracting wildlife

To attract wildlife, site the pond in an open, sunny position, away from overhanging trees. Slope one edge of the pond, like a beach, so that creatures can get in and out easily. If you can, make the pond at least 1 m (3¼ ft) square and as deep as possible. If the pond is too small, particularly too shallow, it will quickly heat up giving problems with algae and pond weed. The water in new ponds will turn green initially, but it will soon settle down and clear if you grow oxygenating plants in it. Early spring is the best time to create a pond.

Types of pond liner

Traditionally, ponds were lined with concrete, which can be messy to use and needs shuttering for a good finish. Concrete often cracks after a few years, and although it is still used for some formal ponds, it is not really suitable for a natural or wildlife pond.

Rigid plastic liners are preformed into various shapes and are widely available. Good-quality plastic liners can be expensive, but they are easy to install and maintain.

Liners made from butyl rubber, are probably the best and easiest to use, especially for wildlife ponds. The best butyl will last for 25 years or more, although less expensive material is available but will not last as long. The great advantage of butyl is that it is flexible and can be used for any size and shape of pond. Make sure you buy enough for the depth of the pond and to extend beyond the perimeter. Use a proprietary underlay under the butyl for best results.

Digging and lining a pond

To create a butyl-lined pond dig a hole slightly larger than the pond is to be to allow for the protective underlay and the liner. Create a shallow shelf along one edge for plants. When you have excavated the hole, go over the surface carefully to remove sharp stones and roots, which may puncture the liner. Use a spirit level to check that the sides are level by laying a piece of timber

Left Having a pond on your allotment will encourage wildlife like frogs, which will help to control pests.

Lay the liner loosely over the hole, making sure there is plenty of overlap all round. Place large stones around the edges to hold it in place and to allow the liner to slip gently into the hole. Move the stones as necessary to hold the liner again, and then begin to fill the hole slowly with water. The weight of water will pull the liner into the hole. If you want to plant directly into the pond put some soil in the bottom at this stage. When the pond is half-full, check the level of the sides again and adjust if necessary.

When the pond is full, check the level again – you cannot do this too often – and bury the edges of the liner under turf or soil to prevent sunlight damaging it. Plant around and in the pond to make it look natural.

across the pond from end to end and side to side. If necessary, add or remove soil. Cover the surface with a 5 cm (2 in) layer of builder's sand over the inside of the hole and cover this with an underlay, such as old carpet or proprietary pond underlay. Do not use cardboard or newspaper, which will rot away.

techniques and tasks

While you are caring for your allotment throughout the year, there are number of basic techniques and tasks that you will need to carry out at different times. After you have cleared and prepared your allotment, sowing and planting your crops will be the first major tasks. Next come all the tasks associated with continuing care and maintenance, such as watering, feeding, mulching, getting rid of weeds, attracting beneficial wildlife, pruning and training and providing plant supports.

Sowing

Growing from seed is the simplest and most straightforward way of growing your plants. Even after 30 years of gardening, I have never lost the thrill of seeing seeds germinating. Those first green shoots pushing through the soil are a wonderful sight and a promise of things to come. However, seeds need the right conditions to germinate and grow well, and it is up to you to provide those conditions. Seeds need warmth and moisture to germinate, and if you get the combination wrong the seeds won't grow properly.

Sowing outdoors

Because it requires no specialist equipment, perhaps the simplest way of all to sow seeds is to sow outdoors. There are several ways of doing this, but first you must prepare the soil properly. The soil needs to be broken down to a fine tilth (a fine, crumbly structure) and you do this with a fork, before levelling it with a rake. If you can mulch the area for sowing the autumn before with leaf mould or fine compost, so much the better, because this will improve the soil structure at the surface where seedlings need it most. Of course, if the allotment is new to you, this won't be possible.

Don't work on the soil if it's too wet, because this will ruin the structure and the soil will bind into large clods, which are useless for sowing into. Make the seedbed by giving a final rake to level it and, if necessary, firm the soil beforehand.

Avoid sowing too early in the year; the soil temperature needs to be a minimum of 7°C (45°F). For tender crops, such as courgettes or sweet corn, wait until the soil reaches about 10°C (50°F). A soil thermometer is a useful piece of kit, but just look at existing plants in and around your allotment. If buds on plants and in hedgerows are beginning to open it is a sure sign that the soil is warming up and is ready for seed sowing.

Below Pouring the seeds from a packet directly into your hand before you sow them allows you to assess their size and condition.

Below To provide the correct conditions for seeds to germinate, rake the soil to a fine tilth – a fine, crumbly structure.

Station sowing: Station sowing, which is sometimes known as space sowing, involves sowing two or three seeds at the final planting distance or station. It reduces the need for thinning out because only one or two seedlings need be removed, and it saves on the number of seeds you use.

Thinning out: You need to reduce the number of seedlings in beds or containers to allow the remainder space to develop properly. The process of removing individual seedlings is known as thinning out, and it is done once the seedlings have germinated and begun to compete with one another for light, moisture and nutrients. If you leave them unthinned the seedlings will become weak and leggy and be next to useless. Initially, thin out so that the leaves of the seedlings don't touch. Later, thin to 8 cm (3 in) or to 15 cm (6 in), depending on the crop's requirements. Look on the back of seed packets to get the final spacing for growing on. Larger seeds, such as peas and beans, are easy to sow singly at the correct space and shouldn't need thinning out. They are usually station sown (sown at the correct spacing). Peas are usually sown around 5–8 cm (2–3 in) apart and runner beans are usually sown one seed at the base of each cane used to support them.

Sowing spinach in drills

Sowing in drills is the easiest way to sow seeds. All it involves is taking out shallow v-shaped trenches, or drills, with a cane or your finger. This system of sowing has the advantage that when seeds germinate they are easily distinguished from emerging weeds, because the crop seedlings are in straight rows.

1 Rake the soil to a fine tilth and make shallow drills with a piece of wood.

2 Take out the drills in a fan shape to add interest. This is a good technique to use on the bed system (see pages 34–5).

3 Spinach seeds are a reasonable size and can be sown easily at regular spacings of approximately 2.5 cm (1 in).

4 Pick up and reposition any seeds that land too close to the previously placed seed to ensure adequate room for the plants when they begin to grow.

5 Cover the seeds lightly with soil, then firm the soil with the palm of your hand. The seeds will germinate in two or threes weeks making an attractive pattern.

Sowing indoors

Starting crops indoors can give you a head start on growing outside, and if you have a greenhouse or a cold frame you can start earlier, growing the plants on without any danger that they will get frosted. Even if you have a greenhouse, sowing seeds in a propagator on a windowsill will save on your heating bills. Seeing those first seeds germinating when all is cold and miserable outside is one of the great thrills of gardening.

A heated propagator for starting seeds off is not essential, but it will give seedlings the best start. There are many types available, and you can choose any model and size that appeals to you and that you can afford. Remember, however, that it needs to be capable of maintaining temperatures of 18–21°C (64–70°F).

Containers: Containers come in all shapes and sizes, but an ordinary seed tray or plenty of small pots will be ideal. Whatever you choose to sow seeds in, whether it be old margarine or ice cream tubs, make sure they are perfectly clean and that there are adequate drainage holes in the base.

Composts and sowing: There are several types of organic seed compost and multipurpose compost available for growing seeds in, and it is a case of trying different kinds until you find the one that suits you best. Always use peat-free formulations. Water the compost before sowing, otherwise the seeds can get washed deeper into the compost and can fail to germinate.

Pricking out: Seedlings that have grown in seed trays or small pots will need pricking out (moving to more spacious pots) when they get to the stage of having made two complete seed leaves (cotyledons). This will give the young plants room to develop into sturdy plants that can be transplanted outside. Prick out so the seedlings are 2.5–5 cm (1–2 in) apart in each direction and water in. Shade the seedlings from strong sunshine for a few days until they become established.

Hardening off: Before you can plant young plants outside they will need hardening off – that is, being acclimatized to outdoor growing conditions. If you haven't got a greenhouse, put the plants outside for a few hours during good weather and bring them in later in the day. Gradually increase the time the plants stay outside, over a period of about a week, and by then they will be used to outdoor conditions. If you have a cold

frame, gradually leave the cover open for longer periods. Don't plant out tender crops, such as tomatoes and courgettes, until the threat of frost has passed.

Watering and planting: Before you plant out the seedlings make sure that all your trays and pots of plants are well watered. If the compost is dry before planting out it will stay dry, no matter how much moisture there

Cell trays

Cell trays are seed trays with individual compartments, so they are useful for pricking out seedlings (see above). They are ideal for sowing larger seeds, such as peas and beans, and for multiple sowing, which involves sowing five or six seeds to a cell. This has the advantage that seedlings don't need to be thinned.

However, the main advantage of cell trays is that once the seedlings grow on there is minimal disturbance of the roots when you come to plant them out. This means the plants get off to a better start as their growth is not checked or interrupted. Insert the seedlings so that the seed leaves are just touching the compost in the cell then water them in.

Cell trays are great to use when sowing deep beds. For instance, sowing onions in this way means you get five or six plants in a cluster and a heavier overall crop compared to setting out the plants individually.

Sowing larger seeds

You can sow large seeds, such as peas, in trenches that should be about 15 cm (6 in) wide and 2.5 cm (1 in) deep. Most seeds don't need burying deeply, just cover with soil to about twice their own depth. Even larger seeds, like runner beans and broad beans, need to be sown a little deeper, about 5 cm (2 in) deep.

Above You can use all sorts of containers for sowing seeds. Just make sure you puncture the base to make drainage holes if they don't already have ready-made holes.

Below right A cold frame for hardening off young plants before planting out. Tender crops, such as melons, can be grown in it later in the season.

is in the soil. And it is important to water in well after planting out, particularly where you have to disturb plant roots, such as when removing plants from a seed tray. This applies to all plants. Final planting distances will vary, depending on the crops you are growing and whether you are growing in traditional rows or in the bed system (see pages 34–5).

Buying young plants

If you don't have the facilities or the inclination to raise your own plants from seeds you can buy them. You may be able to buy organically grown transplants from a mail order company, or even be lucky enough to have a local source, but if not, go to your nearest garden centre. What we want is for you to be as organic as you can manage, even if this means you need to buy non-organic plants or seeds to get started. In time you can source organic plants or harvest seeds from our own plants.

Easy-to-grow vegetables

Beetroot

FAMILY:
Chenopodiaceae
SOW:
Spring to summer
HARVEST:
Summer to autumn

Broad Beans

FAMILY:
Papilionaceae
SOW:
Spring and autumn
HARVEST:
Summer to autumn

Brussels Sprouts

FAMILY:
Brassicaceae
SOW:
Spring
HARVEST:
Autumn to winter

Cabbage

FAMILY:
Brassicaceae
SOW:
Spring to summer
HARVEST:
Summer to winter

Carrots

FAMILY:
Apiaceae
SOW:
Spring to summer
HARVEST:
Summer to autumn

Celery, self-blanching

FAMILY:
Apiaceae
SOW:
Spring
HARVEST:
Summer to autumn

Leeks

FAMILY:
Alliaceae
SOW:
Spring
HARVEST:
Autumn to winter

Lettuce

FAMILY:
Asteraceae
SOW:
Spring to summer
HARVEST:
Summer to autumn

Onion

FAMILY:
Alliaceae
SOW:
Spring to summer
HARVEST:
Summer to autumn

Peas

FAMILY:
Papilionaceae
SOW:
Spring to summer
HARVEST:
Summer to autumn

Potatoes

FAMILY:
Solanaceae
SOW:
Spring
HARVEST:
Summer to autumn

Pumpkins

FAMILY:
Cucurbitaceae
SOW:
Spring
HARVEST:
Autumn

Radish

FAMILY:
Brassicaceae
SOW:
Spring to summer
HARVEST:
Summer to autumn

Rhubarb

FAMILY:
Polygonaceae
SOW:
Spring
HARVEST:
Summer

Runner Beans

FAMILY:
Papilionaceae
SOW:
Spring
HARVEST:
Summer to autumn

Shallots

FAMILY:
Alliaceae
SOW:
Spring
HARVEST:
Summer

Spinach

FAMILY:
Chenopodiaceae
SOW:
Spring to summer
HARVEST:
Summer to autumn

Tomatoes

FAMILY:
Solanaceae
SOW:
Spring
HARVEST:
Summer to autumn

Turnip

FAMILY:
Brassicaceae
SOW:
Spring to summer
HARVEST:
Summer to autumn

Watering your allotment

Using a lot of water for plants these days is a contentious issue, because our ever-changing climate is affecting water supplies. We should do all we can to conserve it. There are many ways to save and use less water and some of these are discussed below. Many areas will suffer from hosepipe bans, both now and in the future, making it even more important that you and your allotment are prepared.

Conserving water

The more you can conserve moisture in the soil the better. Not only will you need to use less water, but you will spend less time actually watering your plants. Only water the most vulnerable plants – those that have just been planted out and newly planted fruit trees and bushes. Older, established plants will generally survive without watering regularly except in exceptionally dry conditions. There is an argument that only food crops should be watered and that ornamental plants should be left to fend for themselves.

Also you can conserve moisture in the soil, by keep all digging to a minimum and not digging during dry spells. This will reduce the exposure of the soil to the drying effect of the sun and wind.

Water amounts

If you have to water make sure that you allow enough for the plants' needs. There is no point giving small amounts every day or two. This is wasteful and does the plants no good at all, as it simply encourages the roots to come nearer the surface in search of it. It is much better to water a small area thoroughly when needed.

When to water

The best time to apply water is in the evening or very early morning. At these times, when it is cooler, there is less evaporation and there is less chance of the plants' leaves being scorched by strong sunlight.

Shade Young plants, such as seedlings and newly transplanted seedlings, require shade, especially if the sun is strong, as this reduces the amount of water they need. Shade netting draped over plants or seed drills is an ideal way to protect plants from the harsh sun.

Mulching This is a vogue word in gardening, but all it means is covering the surface of the soil to prevent moisture loss. Mulching with certain materials is also a way of adding organic matter and nutrients to the soil (see pages 54–5).

Seep hoses It it is important to get the water to where it is most needed, which is at the roots of the plants. The trouble with watering with a hosepipe, or even a watering can, is that a lot of the water is lost through evaporation. If you have an available tap seep hoses are a good way of getting round this problem, because the water is released very gradually. Attach the seep hose to a hose and lay the it on, or just below, the surface of the soil so that the water oozes out from the pores in the pipe, getting straight to the roots. Seep hoses are usually made from recycled rubber reducing the amount of rubber that is thrown away.

Shelter Some shelter, in the form of a shelter belt of fencing or fruit trees and bushes on the windward side of the allotment, will reduce wind flow over the allotment. This will help reduce the amount of evaporation from foliage, further reducing the amount of extra water that plants need.

Weeds Weeds undoubtedly take a lot of moisture from the soil, so keep them under control. Hoe them off in dry weather and they will shrivel up in the sun.

Water butts Use as many water butts as possible to catch water from the roof of the greenhouse and shed, if you have either or both on your allotment. Butts can store a lot of water over a season. Some local authorities sell them at a reduced rate (along with compost bins) to encourage their use. You can usually buy them from garden centres. Butts are often made from recycled plastic, which would normally end up in a landfill site.

Feeding

Like humans, plants need to eat. If you are using compost and other organic matter and growing green manures, there should be no need for supplementary feeding. However, supplementary feeding is useful at the start, if the plot has not been looked after well and plants are not growing well. Also, if you are short of organic matter, applying organic fertilizers will give the plants the nutrients they require. The only other time you should need to apply fertilizers is if plants show signs of nutrient deficiency.

Organic fertilizers

Organic fertilizers can be of animal, plant or mineral origin. The nutrients they contain are released slowly as the fertilizer is broken down by microorganisms in the soil. Slow-release fertilizers produce sturdier plants that are less susceptible to attack from pests and disease; chemical fertilizers encourage a quick burst of growth producing weaker plants.

Some organic fertilizers, such as pelleted chicken manure and seaweed meal contain a range of plant nutrients, while others like rock phosphate contain more specific nutrients. When applying fertilizers always wash your hands afterwards.

If you are not keen on using animal-derived plant fertilizers there are a number of plant-based alternatives on the market. A good general fertilizer is one based on lucerne, vinasse, rock phosphate, molasses and sugars. Comfrey pellets that contain all the major nutrients and trace elements are also available. Look in an organic garden catalogue for these and other suggestions.

- **Bonemeal** is a popular fertilizer, high in phosphates, which stimulate root growth. Always wear gloves when you are applying it.
- **Dolomitic limestone** is used to raise the pH in the soil either to make it more alkaline or less acid. Always test your soil before applying limestone (see page 27). Dolomitic lime also contains calcium and magnesium.
- **Potash (organic garden)** is a soluble potassium from an organic source and is ideal for correcting deficiencies of potash. It is particularly suited for deficiency in tomatoes and fruit.
- **Rock potash** is an alternative source of phosphate and is a good non-animal alternative to bonemeal when a shortage of phosphate is identified – when there is poor growth and leaves turn bluish green.
- **Seaweed meal** is a slow-acting plant food that is particularly rich in trace elements. It is a soil conditioner that helps to build up the humus structure of the soil. Apply to the soil up to three months before sowing or planting.

Left Seaweed meal is a good, balanced organic fertilizer to use as a supplementary feed.

Left When peas have died down the tops can be cut off. Leave the roots to return nitrogen to the soil. However, remove the tops because there is little nutrient left in these to go back into the soil.

Below Using foliar feeds gives plants a quick boost. Do not apply on hot, sunny days as the water droplets may scorch the foliage.

- **Wood ash** is also a good source of potassium and a small amount of phosphate. The nutrient content will vary, however, depending on the material burned. Wood ash is best put on the compost heap.

Applying fertilizers

Apply organic fertilizers a few days up to a couple of weeks before sowing or planting. This is because the nutrients are released more slowly than by other fertilizers, so they will be available to the plants at the precise time they require them.

It is impossible to give here precise details of the amounts of fertilizer you should apply, as so much depends on your soil and how well the plants are growing. The best way to find out how much to apply is to add fertilizer only if growth is unsatisfactory or if plants appear to have specific deficiencies, such as a lack of nitrogen resulting in yellowing leaves. Apply fertilizers according to the manufacturers' instructions.

Foliar feeds

Foliar feeds are a quick way to apply nutrients, although the results can be short-lived and the process will have to be repeated often. Liquid seaweed, for example, is a rapid-acting tonic for any plant suffering from nutrient deficiency of trace elements. You should regard foliar feeding as a supplement to feeding the soil. To apply a foliar feed spray the leaf surface, tops and underside, until the fertilizer liquid begins to drip off.

When to feed

If plants are growing healthily there is no need to add fertilizers of any sort to the soil. If you apply plentiful supplies of organic matter each year this should replace most of the nutrients lost through plant uptake and leaching from the soil. However, if you are growing intensely on your allotment or you are growing plants in containers, you may find it necessary to replace some of the nutrients taken out of the soil by the plants.

Mulching

Mulching is a method of controlling weeds, improving soil structure and retaining moisture in the soil. Mulches also protect the soil surface from the elements, and depending on what type of material you use, they can provide nutrients for plant growth. There are many types of mulching materials available from organic to inorganic, so the one you choose will depend on what you want it to do; whether you are concerned about its appearance; and whether you want something that is quick and effective. Here we look at mulches used for weed control. For mulches that will return nutrients to the soil see pages 28–9.

Materials

There are many materials that you can use as a mulch, and some are more attractive than others. On an allotment, where the emphasis is on production not appearance, go for the most efficient method. The best time to put down a mulch is in spring when the soil is still moist. If you are putting down a mulch at any other time of the year make sure you thoroughly water the soil beforehand – a mulch is just as good at keeping water out as keeping it in the soil. Avoid mulching cold soil, unless you want to keep it cold or are using polythene to warm it.

Black polythene Black polythene is one of the most effective materials for mulching to eradicate perennial weeds. When the polythene is laid on the soil no light can get at the weeds and so they die. You will need to anchor the polythene with bricks or bury the edges in the soil. Cut X-shaped slits in the polythene if you want to plant through this mulch.

Paper and biodegradable polythene Use these materials in the same way as black polythene, although biodegradable polythene tends to deteriorate into unsightly strips. If you use tough brown paper, which can be bought from garden centres, you can roll it on to an area of ground and anchor it by burying the edges in the soil. As with polythene, to plant your crops cut slits in the paper. After you have harvested the crops either dig the paper in or put it on the compost heap.

Newspaper Newspaper is a cheap alternative mulch, but it is time-consuming to lay. You will need about six to eight layers of paper, and you will have to anchor them in the soil using grass cuttings, leaf mould or straw. The paper will last for quite some time, but it will not rot down until you tear it into strips and put it on the compost heap. Mix it in with plenty of other material to hasten the decomposing process.

Left Strawy well-rotted manure or compost spread between crops will help retain moisture in the soil. Remove weeds before spreading the material.

Mulching with newspaper

1 Put down at least 6–8 layers of newspaper. Soaking it in water first will prevent it from being blown away. Make sure the layers are well overlapped to ensure the entire surface is covered.

2 Spread grass clippings, straw or compost over the dampened paper to keep it in place. The result is attractive and will keep down weeds, and will help retain moisture in the soil.

Cardboard This can cost nothing if you go to your local recycling centre or tip and retrieve it, and it is a useful material for one entire season. If you can, use plain brown cardboard, not the type that has colourful logos and messages printed on it or that has a glossy finish. Cardboard can look unattractive, but if you cover it with straw or hay it will look better. They will also keep the cardboard in place. You can plant vigorous crops, such as pumpkins and marrows, through cardboard.

Compost and manures Used as mulch, these two organic matters will return nutrients to the soil, making them available to plants. Try to use as much garden compost as you can – a layer 5 cm (2 in) thick, at least – as often as you can.

Shredded prunings You can hire or buy shredders that will shred most woody prunings. It's best to compost the prunings for a while before using them as a mulch, as they can leach nutrients from the soil. They are not suitable for mulching vegetable crops, but they are useful for pathways between rows of fruit crops.

Grass cuttings Most allotments have some grass on them, even if it's just a small lawn outside the shed or a pathway or two. If you apply grass cuttings thickly enough straight from the mower's grassbox – about 5 cm (2 in) depth – they will be effective at keeping weeds under control. Alternatively, of course, put them on the compost heap to rot down or use them over newspaper or cardboard.

Biodegradable materials New biodegradable materials, such as hemp fibre and hessian, can also be used. Keep these materials in place with wire pegs or spreading straw, for example, over them.

Green waste compost Many local authority and council recycling centres compost garden waste. This is a great source of organic matter and is available relatively cheaply – sometimes for free. In most cases you will have to transport the material to the allotment yourself, but it is worth making enquiries about this, because you might able to organize a bulk delivery if several allotment-holders order some.

Green manure An effective way to control weeds and return nutrients to a patch of bare soil is the use of green manure (see page 31). It will also help to improve the soil structure and ultimately increase yields.

Weeding

Weeds can be troublesome because they not only compete for light but also take moisture and nutrients from the soil. The key to weed control is to take measures when the weeds are small and before they have a chance to set seeds. Perennial weeds, such as ground elder and bindweed, are difficult to get rid of because they grow so rapidly. Annual weeds are easy to control because, as with hardy annual flowers, they grow, flower, set seeds and die in one season. The mulching methods described on pages 54–5 will help to control weeds, but here are a few other methods as well.

Hand-weeding

This is an easy method of organic weed control. Use a hoe between rows of crops and around fruit trees and bushes. On deep beds it is better to hand-weed with a small fork, but if crops are florishing on a well-planted deep bed you shouldn't really have to do much weeding.

The quickest way to control weeds on your allotment, if growing in traditional rows, is with a Dutch hoe. It is an effective tool for controlling weed seedlings and taking the tops off annual weeds. You can also use the hoe to knock off the tops of perennial weeds, but this way of controlling them may take several years to take effect.

Heat

You can use a thermal weeder to kill seedling weeds. These are usually powered by paraffin or gas, and the idea is not to burn the weeds, but to apply sufficient heat to make them begin to wilt, which is enough to kill them. It is a good idea to go over seedbeds with a thermal weeder before you start sowing to kill any weed seeds that may be on or near the surface.

Digging out

This is a labour-intensive way of weeding, and it can be quite daunting to clear a whole allotment, but it is very satisfying when you have done it. There will, inevitably, be a mixture of annual and perennial weeds (see opposite), and it is the perennial weeds that are the most difficult to treat. When you dig these out it is vital to remove every piece of root to avoid regrowth.

Mulching

Mulching is a good way of controlling and clearing weeds, but on an overgrown allotment you may have to cut down all the topgrowth before you can apply a mulch. On a heavily overgrown plot, you will have greater success with black polythene, which will exclude all light from the area more effectively (see pages 54–5). To prevent weeds getting established on bare patches of soild use green manures (see page 31).

Left If allowed to self-seed, weeds such as dandelion will quickly colonize an allotment.

Perennial weeds

Listed below are some common perennial weeds. They are in effect herbaceous perennials in that they have extensive root systems that remain alive in soil over winter when the topgrowth has died down, and they last for many years. Any piece of root, however small, left in the ground will regrow.

Ground elder
(*Aegopodium podagraria*) is a difficult weed to control because it has creeping underground stems that produce new leaves at every joint. Control by persistent, regular, hoeing or dig out every piece of root. Cover with a membrane, such as black polythene or paper or biodegradable polythene, to exclude light.

Field bindweed
(*Convolvulus arvensis*) is a most pernicious weed, which is difficult to control because it has deep roots. Dig out as many of the roots as possible, although it may take several years to eradicate these weeds entirely.

Creeping buttercup
(*Ranunculus repens*) is common on most plots. It spreads by runners, similar to strawberries. Use a hoe when the plants are small, but otherwise dig out all the roots.

Blackberry or bramble
(*Rubus fruticosus*) is a prickly customer that produces edible fruits, but it can take over the allotment if you let it get out of control. Digging out young plants is the easiest method, but wear gloves when you are dealing with overgrown patches because the thorns are sharp.

Dandelion
(*Taraxacum officinale*) is one of the most easily recognized weeds. It has a long taproot, which makes it easier to dig out than other weeds, but you must remove all the roots. Dandelions also seed freely, so don't let them get to the flowering stage.

Stinging nettles
(*Urtica dioica*) are valuable for wildlife, particularly butterflies, but they can be a pain (literally) on your allotment. Digging out is the best way to control stinging nettles. If you want to attract wildlife leave a small patch behind the shed or somewhere out of the way, but you will still need to keep them under control.

Couch grass
(*Elymus repens*) is a common allotment weed that can be difficult to control, particularly among permanent crops. The best way to control couch grass is digging out as much of the root as possible and preventing the plants making above ground growth.

Dock
(*Rumex sp.*) produces distinctive, large, mid-green leaves. Docks are hard to control as they have a long main taproot. Even the smallest piece of root left in the soil will regrow.

Below Perennial weeds have to be dug out. Make sure you get all the roots as they will regrow if any part remains in the soil.

Attracting beneficial wildlife

There is no doubt that an allotment teeming with wildlife is a pleasant place to spend time, and, if you can get a good variety of birds and other insects into your allotment they will certainly help in keeping pests under control. The key to attracting wildlife is to create the right habitat and conditions, and even on an allotment you can go a long way to providing that environment. You will be pleasantly surprised at just how quickly those beneficial creatures will appear. Remember that weeds can be good for wildlife, too.

Food for wildlife

Of course, birds are going to do their best to eat the fruits you grow for yourself. Strawberries, for example, are as irresistible to birds as they are to us, so you will have to net them, but make sure the netting is secure otherwise birds will get tangled up and suffer serious injury or even death. Wildflowers attract wildlife and provide food in the form of seeds for birds and insects. It is better, whenever possible, to grow flowers that will attract wildlife and provide them with food. For instance, sunflowers are great plants for providing seeds for birds in winter. It's easy to fit a few plants in a corner somewhere.

Cultivated flowers Not only a delight to look at, cultivated flowers are invaluable for attracting beneficial wildlife. Many insects will come to feed on the nectar and pollen the flowers produce – then they go on to eat the pests on the plot. These insects are part of the food chain and they will attract birds and other predatory insects to feed, helping to control pests. See page 61.

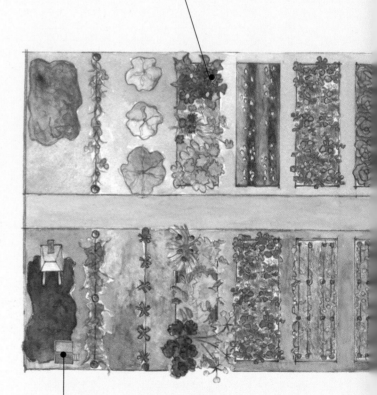

Shelters One of the most important ways to attract wildlife on to your allotment is to provide them with a home. Hedgehog boxes are good because hedgehogs eat a tremendous number of slugs and other pests. Site the box in a corner of your allotment plot where the hedgehogs will be undisturbed. Bird nesting boxes are important, too, and are easy to make with quick results. Put one on the shed on the shady side so that it doesn't heat up too much, and remember to clear it out every autumn.

Compost bins Even your compost bins are good for attracting wildlife. Creatures, such as lizards, can be found in them.

Water Perhaps the most important thing as far as wildlife is concerned. Providing water is essential if you want to attract animals and birds. Even a simple bird bath will bring birds from far and near, and a small pond is even better. Dragonflies will be attracted to a half-barrel pond, so you don't need a vast pond.

Wildflowers Growing a patch of wildflowers is a joy, even on an allotment. It needn't take up much space but will repay the use of it a hundred-fold by the insects and creatures it will attract. A corner at one end of the allotment will be quite adequate.

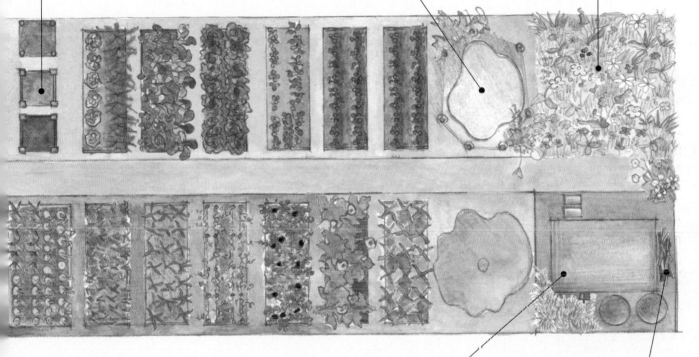

Shed The shed is not only a home for gardeners but to wildlife, too. While you're sitting drinking your tea, insects and others creatures will be hiding away in corners, perhaps behind old bags of potting compost or in a stack of pots.

Log pile A log pile is a useful home for creatures such as frogs, hedgehogs, newts and beetles. A few logs from pruning old shrubs left in a pile by the shed will be an ideal home for these creatures, but leave them undisturbed or they will look elsewhere for a quieter place to live.

Keeping plants healthy

The aim of keeping your plants healthy is to maintain a balance between friend and foe, pests and diseases, and their natural enemies. It can be difficult to maintain this balance on an allotment where so many different crops are being grown in close proximity, but with vigilance, problems can be nipped in the bud before they get out of control. Using organic management techniques will help to create this balance, plus growing a diversity of plants to attract wildlife will help encourage predators to polish off the pests that love to eat your crops, too. Here we provide you with some ways to keep your plants healthy.

Know your plot

Get to know your plot and plants so you can spot problems early. There is nothing like getting down on your knees, in among your plants. This way you get to know them intimately and you see how well your plants are growing. Looking after your soil will encourage plants to grow well and shrug off problems as they produce vigorous growth that is resistant to attack by pests and disease (see pages 146–51).

Identify problems

Take time to identify problems so you know what you are dealing with. Some of the problems you will come across are dealt with in this book, but by necessity we can't cover all of them. If you cannot identify a particular problem consult a reference book or contact an organic gardening establishment for advice.

Good hygiene

It is always a good idea to practise good hygiene on your plot. Clear away any plant debris, as it can encourage diseases and pests. Most of it, except woody material, can be consigned to the compost heap. If you see signs of disease or pest damage on plants, cut off the infected parts when you see them and dispose of them either on the compost heap or, for persistent diseases, such as clubroot of brassicas, burn them. When using seed trays and pots, perhaps to raise young plants on the windowsill at home, ensure these are thoroughly cleaned before use.

Physical barriers

There are many physical barriers that can be used to reduce attack from pests and diseases. Horticultural fleece is a popular choice for covering crops. However, it can cause problems encouraging diseases, such as *botrytis* (grey mould), in the warmer, moist conditions under it because of the reduced ventilation. From time to time lift the fleece to allow some ventilation – this is a risk as some pests may get in, but is important if your plants are to grow well in warmer conditions. Despite the reduced ventilation, horticultural fleece is good for keeping pests, such as flea beetle off turnips and radishes, and prevents cabbage white butterflies from laying their eggs on the undersides of brassica leaves.

Above A piece of netting supported on scraps of wood gives perfect protection from birds, but it won't keep off small insect pests.

Flowers to attract wildlife

Daisy family
The simple, open flowers of the daisy family and the tiny flowered umbellifers are most attractive to beneficial insects.

Gaillardias
This group of annuals and short-lived perennials have cheerful daisy-like flowers that are like a magnet to pollinating insects.

Limnanthes
Limnanthese douglassi is a fast-growing annual with yellow flowers and white tips to the petals, and are perfect for attracting bees and hoverflies.

Dahlias
The dwarf, single-flowered cultivar is best for attracting insects from midsummer to late autumn.

Calendula
The pot marigold is an easy-to-grow annual with bright orange or yellow flowers that attract a variety of insects.

Alternatives to horticultural fleece are fine-mesh nettings that give better ventilation, so there are fewer problems, and of course there is ordinary netting for keeping rabbits and birds way.

Cabbage root fly mats
These are put round the base of cabbages, broccoli, cauliflowers and other plants in the brassica family to prevent the cabbage root fly from laying its eggs at the base of the plants.

Grease and grease bands
These can be used to stop pests climbing up the trunk of fruit trees. To avoid damage to the tree, use special fruit tree grease, and on young trees you must use grease bands. Also, if grease is smeared on to a small piece of wood and run along a row of radishes, flea beetles will jump up and stick to the grease – a simple, but effective control.

Pheromone traps
These traps are good for monitoring pest levels and are available for many moth pests. They work by using a sticky board or piece of cardboard and a sachet of the female pheromone. Male moths are attracted by the female scent and get trapped on the sticky card.

Pesticides
There may be occasions when you may have to resort to using an organic spray to control a particular problem if it is getting out of control. However, use any pesticide, even organic ones, in a responsible way. Only spray in early morning or late in the evening when all beneficial insects have gone for the day, and only use according to the manufacturers' instructions.

Biological controls
A few predators and parasites of pests can be bought and introduced to the allotment. There is a parasitic nematode (*Phasmarhabditis hermaphrodita*), which is watered on to the soil to control slugs, but it needs a minimum soil temperature of 5°C (40°F) to work. The range of biological controls available to use is increasing all the time, so check with an organic organization for details and suppliers. You will never get complete control, but pests will be kept to a reasonable level.

Pruning and training

Some gardeners find the prospect of pruning quite daunting. This fear perhaps dates from the bygone days of private estates when head gardeners made pruning seem to be more complicated than it actually is. All that has changed, however, and pruning is something that everyone can and should practise to keep fruit trees and fruit bushes productive and healthy. Don't worry if you make the occasional wrong cut – it probably won't be fatal.

Principles

There are some general principles of pruning that determine the shape and size of a tree and the amount of crop you will get from it. Fruit trees are also often grown in restricted forms, such as cordons, and they need to be trained and pruned in the correct way to keep them to the required size while still producing a heavy crop. Always take your time over pruning as you cannot stick a branch back on. The basic rule to remember is the harder you prune the more vigorous the resulting new growth will be, depending on the time of year.

The pruning requirements for each type of fruit are given here in the individual entries. Pruning that is done on fruit trees in winter will encourage growth, while summer pruning encourages fruiting.

Pruning neglected apple and pear trees

Fruit trees are usually grown on special rootstocks that determine the ultimate size or other characteristics, such as vigour or ability to withstand drought or disease. Suitable rootstocks are given in the individual entries for apples, pears and plums on pages 122–4. Buy new fruit trees from a reputable nursery, where the staff will be able to advise you on the rootstock that is suitable for the conditions in which your new tree will grow.

Pruning neglected fruit trees

Restoring an old neglected fruit tree can seem quite a difficult task, but it is perfectly possible, is actually not a difficult undertaking, and seeing the result is very satisfying. If the tree is so large that it takes up too much space on your allotment and is riddled with pests and diseases it might be better to take it out and start again. If you do this, do make sure that you remove the trunk and roots. However, most fruit trees, of whatever type, can usually be brought back under control with a bit of judicious pruning and training.

Pruning neglected apple and pears

Most apple and pear trees started out as open-centred trees and goblet-shaped bushes. The aim of pruning, which should be done during winter, is to restore the basic framework of branches and to encourage fruiting. When you have finished you want to have four to six main branches spaced evenly around the tree.

- Start by removing all shoots from below the point where the main branches grow out. Also remove any suckers that are growing around the base of the tree.
- Prune out any strong, upright branches, branches that are growing across the centre of the tree, and any other branches that are not required. Take your time choosing the branches you want to remain as once a branch is removed it cannot be put back on again.
- Cut out all dead, damaged or diseased wood. Cut back diseased branches to healthy tissue and burn the material you cut off.
- Remove any shoots in the centre of the tree to open it. Leave the main branches free of sideshoots between the trunk and 60 cm (24 in) along the main branches.
- Work along each of the remaining branches shortening sideshoots and thinning fruiting spurs – small clusters of short stems with fruit buds.

Fruit tree forms

Pyramid

A pyramid tree form has a central trunk with branches trained in increasing length from the top of the tree to the bottom, giving a cone shape. It is suitable for apples, pears, plums and damsons.

Cordon

A cordon is a single-stemmed tree that is usually grown at an angle of 45 degrees to restrict its growth. The flowers and fruits are produced on short spurs along the trunk, which are built up over the years. Cordons with two parallel stems are known as double cordons. It is a good form to use when space is at a premium. A cordon is most suitable for apples, pears and plums.

Spindlebush

This is a cone-shaped tree with the branches trained almost horizontal. This is a highly productive form of training, as the horizontal branches restrict the flow of sap and therefore the tree produces more fruiting buds. If starting with a maiden tree (one year old), tie any side shoots to canes that are pushed into the ground around the tree and its main stake. In subsequent years prune in a similar way to pyramids and standard trees.

Espalier

An espalier is a tree form consisting of a central trunk with horizontal branches from each side and tied to horizontal wires. It usually has three, four or five tiers. There is also a type known as a step-over, which has just one tier. Apples and pears can be grown as espaliers.

Fan

The fan is one of the most decorative forms of fruit tree. The branches radiate from one point, spreading out like fingers. The style can be used for apples, pears, plums, cherries, figs and peaches.

Standard

A standard is the traditional form of tree found in orchards, particularly apples and pears. The crown of the tree is most often above head height, and the trees are grown on fairly vigorous rootstocks. This fruit tree form can get too large for an allotment.

Pruning neglected plums

You can treat overgrown plums in a similar way to apples and pears, but generally the pruning will not need to be as severe. Prune plums between late spring and late summer, after picking the fruit, to avoid the fungal disease silver leaf.

- Reduce the tree to the height and width you require, cutting off larger branches to outward-facing shoots, to open up the centre of the tree.
- Cut out all damaged, dead, crossing, rubbing and diseased branches. Burn any diseased wood.
- Thin out the remainder of the growth so that light and air can penetrate the centre of the tree. Your aim is to create a structure of branches in which none of the shoots is touching.

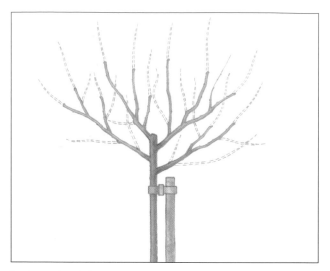

Pruning neglected plum trees

Pruning raspberries

The most delicious of summer fruits are summer raspberries on canes produced in the previous year, and autumn ones from canes produced in the same year. Both types are pruned in different ways.

The best time to cut out old fruiting canes on summer raspberries is just after you harvest the crop. You will need to tie the raspberries to wires supported on posts. This makes it easy to tell the fruiting canes from the new ones, which are the canes that are not tied in.

Autumn-fruiting raspberries are pruned in a different way. They produce fruit on the current year's growth so are best pruned by mid-winter, when all the canes should be cut back to ground level. A few later cropping varieties, such as Autumn Bliss, can be left until late winter.

Pruning old raspberry fruiting canes

Pruning blackberries

Blackberries can take over an allotment if you let them. They can be painful to train and prune because of their thorns, so if you are planting a new blackberry, choose a thornless cultivar, such as Merton Thornless.

Tie the canes to wires supported on strong posts. After fruiting, prune out the old fruiting shoots and tie in the new ones. Either loosely tie in the new canes to the wires, bunching them together until the old canes are cut out, or, if you have space, tie in the fruiting canes to one side of the support (to make a half-fan) and tie the new canes to the other side of the wires (to complete the fan). All you do then is cut out the old canes, leaving the new ones in place for the following year. Repeat the process each year.

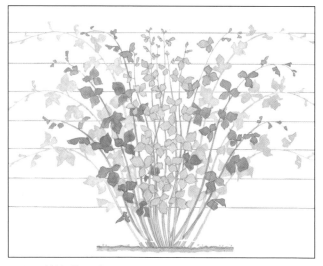

Pruning old blackberry fruiting canes

Pruning red- and whitecurrants

These two fruits are simply variants of the same species, and they are pruned in exactly the same way. They can also be trained as cordons, fans and standards.

Pruning on planting

To create a free-standing bush from a new plant prune all the main stems by about one-third immediately after planting. This will stimulate new extension growth in spring. Cut back any sideshoots to five leaves from their point of growth.

Subsequent pruning

Subsequent pruning consists of the cutting back of side-shoots to five leaves from their point of growth in late mid- to late summer, then cutting back again by about one-third to one or two buds in winter. Keep the centre of the bushes open by cutting out any crossing and touching shoots in winter and maintain a goblet shape. There should a bare stem, about 15 cm (6 in) from the soil surface to the first shoots. Extension growths on the main shoots can be pruned back by about a half to a third, depending on how vigorously they grow in winter.

Pruning blackcurrants

Blackcurrants are not treated in the same way as red- and whitecurrants. They produce fruit on both old and new shoots, so pruning is aimed at promoting new growth while maintaining some healthy old growths.

Prune blackcurrants after fruiting or in winter, after leaf drop, when it is easier to see what you are doing. Cut back a few of the older shoots to the ground every

Above Summer pruning of apples, pears and plums encourages the formation of fruiting shoots or spurs. Do this in late summer.

year. It is inevitable that you will remove some new growths when you do this, but aim to remove about one-third of the bush each year.

Cut out any crossing or touching shoots, leaving the other shoots spaced out to create a balanced looking bush. Start with the branches closest to the soil.

Pruning red- and whitecurrants on planting

Subsequent pruning of red- and whitecurrants

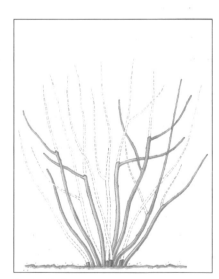

Pruning blackcurrants

Supporting plants

Inevitably some plants on your allotment will need to be supported as they grow. Fruit trees, particularly those grown in restricted trained form and on dwarfing rootstocks, will need staking; and soft fruit, such as raspberries, are best trained on to wires. One of the most popular vegetables of all, runner beans, is the crop that needs most support. Some other vegetables, including peas, will also need some form of structure to grow into.

Fruit trees and bushes

Apples and pears that are grown on dwarfing rootstocks will need staking for most of their lives. When you are planting bare-rooted trees always put the stake or stakes in first after digging the hole, otherwise you might damage the roots when you hammer the stake into the ground. If you are planting a container-grown tree put the stake in at an angle of 45 degrees so that you do not damage the roots.

Put the stake on the windward side so the tree is pushed away from the stake in windy conditions. Trees grown as restricted forms, such as fans, cordons and espaliers, require substantial supports with wooden posts and stout wires. The posts should be set in concrete to make them completely stable. Alternatively, you can use post-holders, which are long metal spikes.

Hammer the holder into the ground and insert the post in the socket. This is easier than mixing up concrete. Raspberries, blackberries, hybrid berries and grapes require similar support systems to espalier and cordon apples and pears, although it need not be as substantial.

Runner and climbing French beans

Runner beans grown up traditional bean poles made from hazelwood always look attractive, especially if you use them on either side of a path and cross over the poles to form an archway. As well as looking good, this method makes it easier to harvest the bean pods as they hang down from the plants. Grow sweet peas with them to make a stunning feature on the allotment.

The simplest way of supporting runner beans is to make a wigwam of five or six poles or bamboo canes, spaced equally apart in a circle, with the tops held firmly together with twine or a special rubber holder.

Whatever support you use, ensure it is strong as there will be a tremendous weight on them once the crops are fully grown and laden with beans.

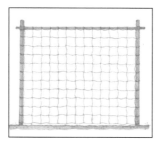

Netting support

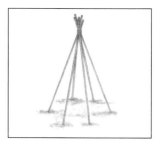

Wigmam support

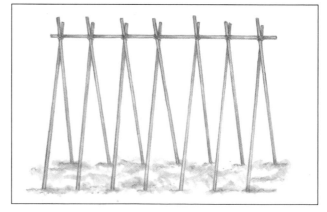

Traditional support for runner beans

Staking rootstocks

Peas

Garden peas will need support. If left unsupported the plants will just trail over the soil, where they will be trodden on or provide an easy meal to slugs and snails. Twiggy sticks, known as pea sticks, are the best support of all, but these are not widely available. Instead, you can buy pea and bean support netting, which is just as effective. Alternatively, you might find that you have something suitable left after pruning overgrown fruit trees and bushes. Well-branched growths from apples, pears or plums will do. Long growth prunings from blackcurrants can also be used, but these may form roots, providing you with new blackcurrant bushes. Whatever you use it should be stong enough to support peas and easy to push well down into the soil.

Broad beans

Taller cultivars of broad beans will also need some support, but here the support method is more utilitarian than visually appealing. Set a couple of canes at either end of a long row and then put a couple more on each side of the row, and wind string around the canes and along the row. The foliage will partly disguise the string, but the aim is to stop the plants flopping on to the soil, which will cause the pods to rot off in wet weather.

Tall-growing vegetables

Tall-growing crops, such as sprouting broccoli and Brussels sprouts, may also need some staking, particularly on exposed sites or in winter when stormy weather is more prevalent. A stout stake, such as a dahlia stake that is 2.5 cm (1 in) thick and 1.2 m (4 ft) long, inserted behind each plant is usually sufficient. Tie the plant securely to the stake with garden twine or a flexi tie, and check these regularly to make sure that the twine or tie is not rubbing the stems or coming loose.

Tomatoes

If you grow the tomatoes on your allotment as cordons (single stemmed) you will have to give them some form of support, as they can produce quite a heavy crop – you can use stout canes or dahlia stakes (see below). If you use canes it is a good idea to hammer two stakes firmly into the ground at each end of the row. Attach a wire between the posts and tie the canes securely to the wire. This may seem unnecessary, but often canes alone are not sufficient to bear the weight of a full, heavy tomato crop.

Twiggy sticks supporting pea plants

Dahlias

Earlier I suggested growing dahlias as cut flowers and to attract beneficial insects (see pages 58 and 61) on to the allotment. Dahlias can make quite large plants and will need support. The taller cultivars are usually supported by stakes, which should be put in before planting. The stake is a piece of wood 2.5 cm (1 in) thick and 1.2–1.5 m (4–5 ft) long. Tie the plant to the stake as it grows. With dwarf cultivars a stout cane is all that you need.

Summer and winter

During the summer a mass of growth will appear around the pruning cuts you made when restoring the basic framework of your apple or pear tree. This growth will need to be managed by removing any shoots in the centre of the tree or below where the main branches start growing. In the winter, thin out shoots at large pruning cuts, leaving any young laterals that will start fruiting in two years.

plant directory

To grow crops well you need to know their individual growing requirements with regard to soil type, sun or shade and water and how they fit into the overall rotation plan. In previous sections of the book we have looked at general conditions and planting and growing techniques, but in this section we look at a wide range of crops in more detail. This is by no means an exhaustive list, but the vegetables, fruit and herbs described here are all tried and tested. Specific cultivars are not suggested, partly because this is a largely personal choice and partly because new variants are becoming available all the time. You will also find that some cultivars do better in some areas than others, and talking to your fellow allotment-holders will be one of the best ways to find out what will grow well on your allotment.

Key

The following symbols are used to indicate the ease of growing and moisture and light requirements of the vegetables, fruits and herbs described in this section.

Ease of growing

 easy to grow

 moderately difficult to grow

 difficult to grow

Moisture requirements

 dry conditions

 moist conditions

 very moist conditions

Light requirements

 full sun

 semi-shade

 shade

Vegetables

Introduction

Growing your own vegetables is one of the most rewarding things to do on your allotment. Most vegetables grow fairly quickly, so you get quick results, which is particularly important for getting children interested in growing their own food. Many children grow up not knowing where their food comes from, but if they are involved in the various stages, from sowing seeds to harvesting their dinner, they will be more appreciative of food and will gain great pleasure and satisfaction from growing it. Of course, this applies to adults, too.

The following descriptions include a note of the different soil conditions required, and this will help when you come to make your crop rotation plan (see pages 24–5). The crops described are, of course, a personal choice, but they are here as examples of what vegetables can be grown, so choose what you like to eat and what you have space for. The vegetables are grouped according to family, and members of the same family often require similar growing conditions.

Members of the beetroot family, *Chenopodiaceae*, are grown for their juicy roots, which are usually dark red, but may be gold and white. The coloured leaves are highly decorative and are also edible when young. The roots can be stored over winter. The so-called leaf beets include perpetual spinach and Swiss and ruby chard. The chards are also highly decorative as well as edible and easy to grow. These crops prefer fertile soil that retains moisture, and all can be grown under cover to extend the period of cropping.

The potato family, *Solanaceae*, includes a wide range of crops. In addition to potatoes, there are tomatoes, peppers and aubergines. Although potatoes prefer cool

Below A well-tended allotment is not only productive but also rewarding to work on and a joy to look at.

conditions, the others prefer warmer conditions. There is a wide choice of varieties of potatoes, far wider than the narrow range available in supermarkets. Home-grown tomatoes, picked straight from the plant, are far better than anything you can buy in the shops. The taste of peppers can range from sweet to blisteringly hot if you grow chilli peppers. Aubergines are becoming more popular and are easy to grow. Both aubergines and peppers grow best under cover.

The carrot family, *Apiaceae*, includes a wide range of crops. The flowers of all members appear as flat clusters, known as umbels, and they are good for attracting beneficial insects to the allotment. Carrots and parsnips are the traditional root crops, but celery and celeriac have distinctive flavours. Florence fennel is an attractive plant, as well as being edible, and you can use both the bulb and the foliage. Although the vegetables in the carrot family have differing soil requirements they are usually grown in the same grouping for rotation because they suffer from similar pests and diseases.

Plants in the onion family, *Alliaceae*, have a distinctive flavour and are ideal for flavouring many dishes. The group includes spring onions, bulb onions, shallots and leeks, as well as the herb, chives. All have attractive flowers if they are left to get to that stage. They are easy to grow, and if you choose varieties carefully you can have onions or other members of this group almost year round. They require good fertile soil, but not too rich, as this can cause soft growth that is more susceptible to attack from pests and diseases.

Members of the marrow family, *Cucurbitaceae*, are vigorous growers with large, attractive leaves. They bear edible, yellow, trumpet-shaped flowers and have a trailing habit of growth. Some, like pumpkins, can trail for some distance and are not for the faint-hearted. You can eat the fruits of all this family when they are young, or you can leave them on the plants until they mature. The fruits are produced in all sorts of shapes and colours. These plants are tender annuals, and you need to start them off indoors in heat to get the best results. Once they get going they need little attention.

The vegetables in the pea and bean family, *Papilionaceae*, are grown for their fleshy pods or seeds. Their great advantage is that they have nitrogen-fixing bacteria in nodules attached to their roots, which return nitrogen to the soil, which is why green manure crops from this family are valuable, too. Apart from dwarf runner beans and dwarf broad beans, all these vegetables will need some support, but they are well worth the effort.

The daisy family, *Asteraceae*, contains a diverse range of vegetables, from lettuces to Jerusalem artichokes, which can grow up to 2.4 m (8 ft) tall. Lettuce, an essential element in any summer salad, is perhaps the most widely grown in this group, and this vegetable is not as boring as it used to be, now that there are many different leaf colours and shapes. All the crops in this group are easy to grow, but some, like Jerusalem artichokes, can become invasive if they not kept in check. These, and globe artichokes, are best grown in a permanent bed or corner of the allotment because they will be there for a long time.

The cabbage family, *Brassicaceae*, is a large and diverse group of vegetables, some of which are part of our staple winter diet, and some, like Brussels sprouts, are an acquired taste. By choosing varieties carefully you can harvest crops from this group throughout the year. Many are especially rich in iron, so are worth growing for that reason alone. They are susceptible to a wide range of pests and diseases, but good growing techniques and strict crop rotation will help keep these in check.

Finally, there is a group of miscellaneous vegetables, such as rhubarb and asparagus, which require permanent positions on your allotment.

from sowing to harvest

7 to 13 weeks.

where to plant

They need a site that is open and sunny, but beetroot will not tolerate an acid soil.

soil preparation

No treatment required if you plant on a fertile soil improved for a previous crop.

sowing and planting

Sow round-rooted cultivars in modules – 2 or 3 seeds per cell – on the windowsill in late winter or early spring. Harden off before planting outside under cloches later in spring. Outside, sow seeds from early spring to midsummer every 10 to 14 days for a succession of roots.

spacing

Spacing varies depending on cultivar, the space you have available and whether you are growing the plants in conventional rows or in a bed system. For rows, space each row 23 cm (9 in) apart and thin seedlings 8 cm (3 in) to 15 cm (6 in) apart. For block planting in beds, plant 12.5–15 cm (5–6 in) apart each way.

care

Water often during hot, dry spells or the roots may become woody. When sown directly outside, thin out seedlings when they have produced 2 seed leaves to around 8 cm (3 in). Later, harvest every other 1, leaving the rest at a final spacing of up to 15 cm (6 in).

problems

Beetroot is usually trouble-free.

harvesting and storage

Harvest roots from about golf-ball size upward. For cylindrical cultivars, harvest when around 2.5 cm (1 in) in diameter. Roots can be left in the ground over winter in milder areas. When harvesting twist rather than cut the tops off. To store roots, harvest in autumn and store in a cool, dark, frost-free place, such as a box of moist sand in the shed.

Beetroot (*Beta vulgaris* subsp. *vulgaris*) is a terrific summer vegetable. It is quick and easy to grow and seeds can be sown over a long period from spring to autumn. You eat the swollen part of the root, which forms at ground level. The roots may be round or cylindrical. The flesh is usually deep red, but some cultivars have yellow or creamy-white flesh, which adds colour and variety to mealtimes. You can cook the roots from fresh or store them over winter for use later in the year. The fresh, young leaves can be eaten as greens.

Beetroot

Spinach

Spinach (*Spinacia oleracea*) is a fast-growing plant that is grown for its highly nutritious leaves. The leaves can be flat or wrinkled depending on cultivar, and can be eaten cooked or raw. It is an acquired taste, but spinach is full of iron and will help make you strong and healthy. Spinach is easy to grow, but does best in cooler, moist conditions. Warm weather causes the plants to bolt (produce seed) at an early stage, sometimes even shortly after the germination stage.

from sowing to harvest
5 to 10 weeks.

where to plant
Spinach prefers slight shade in hot weather making it an ideal crop to grow as an intercrop between slower maturing crops.

soil preparation
Apply a low-fertility soil improver or, on poor soil, a medium-fertility soil improver.

sowing and planting
Sow spinach seeds at intervals of 10 to 14 days from early spring until early autumn. Late sowings will overwinter in milder areas if plants are covered with cloches. Seeds will not germinate above 30°C (86°F). Start off early in modules on the windowsill and plant out under cloches in early spring. Outside, sow thinly in shallow drills. For cut-and-come-again crops – young plants harvested when 10–15 cm (4–6 in) tall, leaving 2.5 cm (1 in) of leaves to re-grow – broadcast sow the seeds in wide, shallow drills about 15 cm (6 in) wide and cover lightly with soil.

spacing
Space traditional rows 30 cm (12 in) apart and thin or plant seedlings at 15 cm (6 in) apart. In beds, sow in short rows 15 cm (6 in) apart and thin to 8–15 cm (3–6 in) apart. Plant transplants 8–15 cm (3–6 in) apart each way.

care
Water well in very dry weather. Keep down weeds between the plants.

problems
Spinach is a fast-growing crop and rarely troublesome, although it can be prone to downy mildew.

harvesting and storage
When plants are around 5 cm (2 in) tall, start picking individual leaves. When 15–20 cm (6–8 in) tall, pull the whole plant out, or cut to 2.5 cm (1 in) above soil level and the plants may resprout. Use fresh or freeze.

from sowing to harvest

8 to 12 weeks.

where to plant

Swiss chard will tolerate salt-laden winds so is good on allotments in coastal areas. It tolerates a little shade.

soil preparation

Apply a low-fertility soil improver if the soil had manure or compost for a previous crop. If not, use a medium-fertility soil improver or a nitrogen-rich organic fertilizer.

sowing and planting

Sow in late winter/early spring in modules, one seed per cell, on the windowsill. The seeds are multigerm (several seeds in a cluster): thin to 1 seedling per cell. Harden off seedlings before planting out in mid- to late spring. Alternatively, leave seedlings unthinned and use as a cut-and-come-again crop. Outside, sow from early spring to late summer. Plants from later sowings will last through most winters.

spacing

In conventional rows space the rows 45 cm (18 in) apart with the plants spaced 23 cm (9 in) apart; in the bed system space at 30 cm (12 in) each way.

care

Water the plants in dry weather and mulch to retain moisture. Most over-wintering crops will withstand winter weather, but if severe weather is forecast cover with cloches or horticultural fleece.

problems

Slugs can be troublesome, as can downy mildew.

harvesting and storage

Picking regularly will promote new growth. Pick leaves from the outside of the plants when they are large enough, usually about 8 weeks after sowing. Harvest sooner, when about 5 cm (2 in) high, for the first cut if using as a cut-and-come-again crop. You can cut off the whole plant leaving about 5 cm (2 in) of stems above soil level. Older leaves become coarse and less appetizing, and more prone to pests and diseases.

This easy-to-grow vegetable (*Beta vulgaris* Cicla Group) is often regarded as a substitute for spinach, but it has a slightly different flavour. It is highly ornamental, with large leaves and broad stems in shades of white, red or yellow. The stems are used in a similar way to celery. Ruby chard has dark crimson leaves and dramatic deep red stems; treat it exactly as you would treat Swiss Chard. If you have a garden at home, grow in an ornamental border for dramatic contrasting foliage effects.

Swiss chard

Spinach beet or leaf beat (*Beta vulgaris* Cicla Group), which is also often known as perpetual spinach, is easier to grow than spinach. It does not go to seed as quickly because it is biennial, and it tolerates cold weather, so will stand through most winters. It is a versatile crop in that you can sow seeds in spring for a summer crop and again in summer for a winter crop. You use it in exactly the same way as spinach. Because it is biennial it will last for 2 years or more, but by then the plants are more prone to bolting (running to seed). It is probably best to treat it as an annual sowing seeds every year.

from sowing to harvest

8 to 12 weeks.

where to plant

Spinach beet will tolerate coastal conditions and some shade. It is a good winter crop, but may need some protection with cloches in colder areas.

soil preparation

If soil was improved by applying compost or manure for a previous crop, apply a low-fertility soil improver before sowing or planting. Otherwise, a medium-fertility soil improver, or a low-fertility improver with a nitrogen-rich organic fertilizer will help cropping.

sowing and planting

Sow seeds on your windowsill in early spring in modules, 1 seed per cell. If several seedlings germinate, thin to 1 per cell or plant in clumps if using the bed system. Harden off the seedlings before planting out later in spring. Outside, begin sowing in early spring and continue at 10 to 14 day intervals until late summer. The seeds are large enough to sow 2 or 3 seeds at each station. Thin out or transplant to fill gaps.

spacing

In traditional rows, grow in rows 38 cm (15 in) apart and thin or plant out at 23 cm (9 in) in the rows; in the bed system space at 23 cm (9 in) each way.

care

Water plants in dry weather and mulch to retain moisture using a medium-fertility soil improver to encourage growth.

problems

Spinach beet is fairly robust, but downy mildew may be a problem towards the end of the main growing season. Beet leaf miner may also attack the leaves, causing brown blotches.

harvesting and storage

Harvest leaves from the outside of the plants first. Rejuvenate older plants by cutting back to about 5 cm (2 in) from soil level to encourage new growth.

from sowing to harvest

16 to 24 weeks.

where to plant

Aubergines grow best in a well-drained, fertile soil, preferably in a sheltered part of the allotment. They need good temperatures to crop well, ideally around 25–30°C (75–86°F).

soil preparation

Apply a medium-fertility soil improver before planting.

sowing and planting

Sow aubergines seeds under cover at a temperature of 21°C (70°F) from late winter to early spring. When seedlings are large enough to handle prick out into 10 cm (4 in) pots and keep the plants at 16–18°C (60–64°F) before hardening off and planting in late spring to early summer when the flowers appear and the danger of frost has passed.

spacing

Plant out so there is a distance of 40–45 cm (16–18 in) each way. If using a bed system plant out 30–40 cm (12 16 in) each way.

care

If plants grow tall they may need to be tied to a cane for support. To grow aubergines of a good size, only allow 4–6 fruits per plant. After planting, pinch out the growing tip and this will encourage sideshoots, which in turn encourages more fruits to form. Keep the plants well watered in dry spells.

problems

Aphids can be a problem in the summer.

harvesting and storage

Harvest aubergines when the sun is shining once they have reached the required size. This is usually from midsummer onwards. You can store the fruits for up to 2 weeks in humid conditions, but it is best to use them fresh from the plant.

Aubergine (*Solanum melongena*) is a great crop to grow outside in warmer regions, but in cooler areas the plants may need the protection of cloches. In warmer areas you can grown them as perennials, but most gardeners grow aubergines as annuals, sowing seeds in spring each year. Aubergines are also known as eggplants because of their shape, which can be round, oval or pear-shaped. The colour varies from dark purple to yellowish-green or white.

Aubergines

Peppers (*Capsicum annuum*) are slightly easier to grow than aubergines, particularly in cooler climates, though it is still worth giving your peppers some protection in colder areas. They are tropical plants and need to be started off in heat indoors, but they are well worth the effort. They are annuals, and the fruits, which are usually oblong, can be green, red or yellow. Sweet peppers are excellent raw in salads, but you can eat the mature fruits raw or cooked. Hot, or chilli, peppers are smaller than sweet peppers and considerably hotter, so choose them with care.

from sowing to harvest
20 to 28 weeks.

where to plant
Peppers need a minimum temperature of 21°C (70°F) to produce a good crop. A fertile soil that warms up quickly in spring is essential.

soil preparation
Apply a medium-fertility soil improver in autumn or before planting in early summer.

sowing and planting
Sow seeds when the weather is mild around 20°C (70°F) from mid to late spring. Prick out the seedlings into 8–9 cm (3–3½ in) pots, then when the roots have filled these pots re-pot in larger 10–13 cm (4–5 in) pots. Grow on in a room temperature at a minimum of 12°C (54°F) and plant out the young plants when all the risk of frost has passed.

care
Taller plants may need to be tied to a cane for support. Pinch out the growing tip of the young plants after planting them out. This encourages sideshoots to grow and therefore more fruits to form. Keep the plants well watered when fruiting to avoid blossom end rot.

problems
Aphids and blossom end rot (a black patch that appears on the fruit where the flower dropped from) can be a problem.

harvesting and storage
You can pick sweet peppers while they are still green to encourage more fruits to form or leave them for several weeks to colour and ripen. They will have a sweeter flavour if left to colour. When frost is forecast at the end of the season whole plants can be dug up and hung up in a cool, frost-free place where the fruits will continue to ripen. Harvested peppers can be stored for up to 14 days in cool, humid conditions. Chillies should be left to ripen on the plants. They can be used fresh or hung to dry in a warm dark place then stored, in an airtight jar and kept in a dark place.

from sowing to harvest
13 to 20 weeks.

where to plant
Potatoes prefer an open, sunny site. The ideal soil is humus-rich and preferably acid – a pH of 5–6 is ideal.

soil preparation
Depending on the soil, apply a high-fertility soil improver to the soil before planting or use a medium-fertility soil improver with a nitrogen-rich organic fertilizer in spring.

sowing and planting
Seed potatoes are usually sprouted (chitted) before planting to help them grow more quickly. To chit potatoes put them in a shallow box with the rose end facing upwards – the end with most eyes or buds. Keep the potatoes in a frost-free location in good light until the shoots are about 2.5 cm (1 in) long. Plant out from early to late spring, depending on cultivar, in trenches up to 15 cm (6 in) deep and cover with soil. Another method of growing potatoes is under a straw mulch using the no-dig technique (see page 36).

care
All potato cultivars are prone to frost damage, so have some straw, fleece or newspaper handy and cover young shoots if frost is forecast. Earth up as the season progresses by drawing soil up around the base of the plants. This stops the tubers going green as a result of exposure to the light. The most effective time to water is when the tubers are about the size of marbles, which is usually around flowering time.

problems
Slugs, potato blight and scab can all be troublesome.

harvesting and storage
Early cultivars are harvested from early to midsummer when the plants begin to flower; maincrop cultivars are harvested in autumn when the topgrowth has died; and second earlies are harvested somewhere in between. Harvest on a dry day, and store undamaged tubers in thick paper sacks in a cool, frost-free dark place.

Potatoes (*Solanum tuberosum*) are one of the mainstays of the allotment. They will fully justify the amount of space they occupy on your allotment, though it may not be worth growing maincrop varieties if you don't have much space left after growing your other crops. They are tender perennials with many different cultivars. Early varieties are the best ones to choose because the flavour is generally better and because the ones in the shops are more expensive at the very time the early varieties are ready to crop.

Sweet potatoes (*Ipomoea batatas*) are tender perennials that are usually grown as annuals. They belong to the bindweed family (*Convolvulaceae*), but are included here simply for convenience. Sweet potatoes have a trailing habit and can grow up to 3 m (10 ft) or more. The cultivars vary widely in leaf shape and the size of the tubers. The tubers are cooked, and you can use the leaves in the same way as spinach. Sweet potatoes are subtropical plants and do need warm conditions to grow well, so in colder areas you may need to grow them under cloches.

from sowing to harvest
13 to 20 weeks.

where to plant
Sweet potatoes grow better in an open and sunny but sheltered location.

soil preparation
Depending on the soil, apply a high-fertility soil improver to the soil before planting or use a medium-fertility soil improver with a nitrogen-rich organic fertilizer in autumn or spring.

sowing and planting
Plant the young plants on ridges of soil when the threat of frost has passed. Make the ridges of soil around 25 cm (10 in) high and space between each ridge 30 cm (12 in) apart. Young plants are usually bought from a specialist grower.

spacing
Plant the young sweet potato plants on the ridges about 30 cm (12 in) apart.

care
Keep the soil between the rows weeded until the growth meets. After this the dense foliage will prevent further weed growth. Because sweet potatoes normally grow in subtropical conditions, there should be little need to water them.

problems
Sweet potatoes are susceptible to slugs, wireworms and aphids.

harvesting and storage
Lift the crop when the leaves begin to turn yellow, which is usually 12–16 weeks after planting. Store sweet potatoes in the same way as ordinary potatoes (see page 79).

from sowing to harvest

9 to 20 weeks.

where to plant

Plant out tomatoes in a warm, sheltered spot in full sun with fertile, well-drained soil.

soil preparation

Apply a medium-fertility soil improver. On poorer soils also add a general organic fertilizer.

sowing and planting

Tomatoes need a minimum temperature of 16°C (60°F) to germinate, but seedlings will tolerate cooler conditions. Sowing seeds indoors on the windowsill using a heated propagator is the ideal way to provide sufficient warmth. Sow seeds in spring around 6–8 weeks before the last frost is expected. Prick out seedlings into 8 cm (3 in) pots when large enough to handle, then plant out when the risk of frost has passed in early to late spring. Protect newly planted tomatoes with fleece or cloches if the weather is cold.

spacing

For cordon tomatoes grown in rows spacing the plants and rows 45 cm (18 in) apart. Bush types should be spaced 45 cm (18 in) apart in rows that are 60 cm (24 in) apart. In a bed system all tomato plants and rows of plants are spaced 38 cm (15 in) apart.

care

Once fruit has begun to form ensure plants don't go short of water. With cordon plants pinch out sideshoots as they develop in the leaf axils, and train the growth against canes. Pinch out the growing tips when 4 trusses of fruits have set. Mulch bushy plants with straw or polythene to keep the fruits off the soil.

problems

Tomato blight and blossom end rot (see page 78).

harvesting and storage

Pick fruits as they ripen. At the end of the season pull up whole plants. Hang up in a cool, frost-free place, and the remaining fruits will ripen.

Tomatoes (*Lycopersicon esculentum*) are the crop everyone thinks of in summer. You always seem to find a tomato plant or two in greenhouses or on windowsills. They are treated as annual plants, which originate from tropical areas, so they will need protection in colder areas, although you can grow them outside in most temperate regions. There is a great number of cultivars to choose among, and tomatoes come in shades of red, orange and yellow and all sorts of sizes. There are bush types or cordons, as well as newer cultivars for growing in hanging baskets.

Carrots (*Daucus carota*) are biennials that are normally grown as annuals. They are not difficult to grow on good soil, but stony or heavy clay soils can make them more of a challenge. The feathery foliage is attractive in its own right, but, of course, it is the traditional orange-coloured roots – now also white, purple and yellow – for which they are grown. The roots are normally long and tapered, but some varieties have round roots, which make them better suited to growing in stony or heavy clay soils. There are early and maincrop varieties, and some of these are resistant to carrot fly.

from sowing to harvest
9 to 20 weeks.

where to plant
Sow in an open site with medium to light, stone-free soil. Early and late crops can be grown under cloches to extend the season of cropping.

soil preparation
No additional feeding is necessary on good soils or soil that was manured for a previous crop. Carrots benefit from leaf mould spread over the soil in winter. Don't sow carrots the season after digging in a grazing rye green manure crop.

sowing and planting
Germination is often slow and can be erratic. Round rooted cultivars can be started off in modules. Start sowing early cultivars from early spring and maincrops from mid-spring to early summer.

spacing
Sow thinly in rows 15 cm (6 in) apart and thin earlies to 8 cm (3 in) apart. For a bed system sow broadcast by scattering the seeds in a given area, then thin seedlings to 8–15 cm (3–6 in) apart.

care
Keep the rows weed free and water well in dry weather.

problems
The main problem with carrots is carrot fly. To avoid it grow resistant cultivars and cover the crop with fleece or fine mesh netting. Carrot fly may be attracted by the smell of carrots, so keep thinning to a minimum. Onions may offer some protection, since their smell can confuse this pest. Sow 4 rows of onions to 1 row of carrots.

harvesting and storage
Pull roots while the plants are still young. Maincrop cultivars can be left in the ground over winter in milder areas and used as required. Leaving roots in the ground in heavy clay soils is not advisable, so lift and store in boxes of moist sand.

from sowing to harvest

26 weeks.

where to plant

Celeriac needs a fertile, moisture-retentive soil to do well. It will grow in full sun or semi-shade.

soil preparation

Apply a medium- to high-fertility soil improver or a low-fertility soil improver with a nitrogen-rich organic fertilizer before planting.

sowing and planting

Seeds germinate best at a temperature of 10–19°C (50–66°F). Sow in gentle heat from late winter to early spring and if no heat is available from mid- to late spring. Sow in trays, thinning or pricking out when the seedlings are large enough to handle. Harden off before planting out in late spring or early summer.

care

Keep the plants weed free and well watered throughout the summer. A mulch around the plants will help retain moisture in the soil.

spacing

In traditional rows space plants 30–38 cm (12–15 in) each way but if using a bed system allow 23–30 cm (9–12 in) each way.

care

Water in dry spell and mulch to retain moisture. From midsummer onward remove some lower leaves to expose the crown.

problems

Celeriac can suffer from the same pests and diseases as celery, but is generally trouble-free.

harvesting and storage

Harvest from late summer through to spring, starting when bulbs are large enough to use, about 8–13 cm (3–5 in) in diameter. Either store in the ground, covering the crowns with straw or fleece in severe weather or store in boxes of moist sand in a frost-free place.

This vegetable (*Apium graveolens* var. *rapaceum*) has a swollen root, similar to turnips, but is used in a similar way to celery (see page 84). It is a close relative of celery but is easier to grow. Like celery, it requires a long growing season and plenty of moisture. You can also use the foliage to flavour dishes. The roots are rather ugly but are very nutritious. It is a useful winter vegetable and can be left in the ground over winter in milder areas. If you have problems growing celery, try celeriac instead.

Celery (*Apium graveolens*) is another easy vegetable to grow. If you can't find organic seeds, look for seeds that haven't been treated with a fungicide. Celery can be either blanching or self-blanching. The blanched types are grown in trenches, whereas the self-blanching types are grown on flat ground and are much easier. You can eat the stalks raw or cooked or use the leaves as a seasonal garnish. Although blanching celery does involve a bit more effort, these cultivars tend to have a better flavour than self-blanching celery.

from sowing to harvest

Self-blanching 16 to 24 weeks; blanching 9 months.

where to plant

Celery must have a fertile, moisture-retentive soil.

soil preparation

Apply a high-fertility soil improver or a low- to medium-fertility soil improver with a nitrogen-rich organic fertilizer. For trench (blanching) celery, dig a trench 38–45 cm (15–18 in) wide, 30 cm (12 in) deep in early spring. Mix in to the soil the soil improvers, then fill in the trench to a depth of 10 cm (4 in).

sowing and planting

Sow seeds in trays or modules in gentle heat from early to mid-spring, sowing no more than 10 weeks before the last frost is expected. Thin out seedlings in to pots, or if sown in modules, thin to 1 seedling per cell. Plant out when the threat of frosts has passed.

spacing

Plant trench celery 30–45 cm (12–18 in) apart and allow 1.2 m (4 ft) between trenches. In a bed system, plant self-blanching celery 15–30 cm (6–12 in) apart – closer spacing will give a higher yield of smaller stems.

care

Water frequently during the growing season and remove any discoloured leaves. Begin blanching trench celery once the plants are around 30 cm (12 in) tall by drawing soil up around the plants. Tie newspaper around the plants to prevent soil getting into the crown and causing rotting.

problems

Slugs, celery leaf spot – tiny yellow spots on the leaf surfaces with accompanying grey mould that can occur when the conditions are damp – and calcium deficiency, which is caused by irregular watering.

harvesting and storage

Harvest trench celery in autumn. They will stand over winter, but protect them with straw. Harvest self-blanching types from midsummer to autumn.

from sowing to harvest
10 to 15 weeks.

where to plant
A warm and sunny position with a moisture-retentive soil is ideal for Florence fennel. It does not grow well in heavy, clay soils.

soil preparation
Grow in soil that has been manured or composted for a previous crop. If needed, apply a low-fertility soil improver before planting. A good supply of moisture is essential.

sowing and planting
Sow seeds in a minimum temperature of 15°C (60°F) in biodegradable modules or pots as the roots resent disturbance. Sow seeds from spring to midsummer. Sow 2–3 seeds in 8 cm (3 in) pots or modules from spring to midsummer and thin, leaving the strongest seedling to grow. Plant out young plants, after hardening off, in late spring or early summer when the threat of frost has passed. Seeds can be sown directly in to the soil from mid-spring onward.

spacing
Plant in rows spaced at 30 x 30 cm (12 x 12 in). If using a bed system space at 23 x 23 cm (9 x 9 in).

care
Early and later sowings may need some protection with cloches. Water plants regularly during the growing season to get the maximum bulb size and to avoid the plants from bolting (running to seed). When bulbs are around egg size earth up (pull soil up around the bulbs) to blanch the bulbs keeping them white and succulent.

problems
Slugs and bolting are the main problems. Grow bolt resistant cultivars and do not disturb the roots when transplanting.

harvesting and storage
Cut the bulbs with they are about the size of a tennis ball. Store in the refrigerator for up to 2 weeks.

Florence fennel (*Foeniculum vulgare* var. *dulce*) is grown as an annual and is different from the perennial herb fennel (see page 136). It is not an easy plant to grow but is worth persevering with because of its unique aniseed flavour. You can eat the swollen stem at the base of the plant either raw or cooked. You can also use the fine feathery foliage as a mild flavouring, or garnish. Florence fennel has a short growing season, making it suitable as a catch crop to grow between other, slower maturing crops. It will tolerate a wide range of climates but to grow well needs a good fertile soil.

Florence fennel

Parsnips (*Pastinaca sativa*) are something of an acquired taste, but they are a good winter vegetable. They are easy to grow, but they do need a fairly long growing season. Germination of the seeds can sometimes be erratic, and so it is a good idea to mix seeds of a fast-growing crop, such as radishes (see page 111), with the parsnips so that you can identify the row. Parsnips are often left in the ground over winter because their flavour is improved once they have had frost on them, but in colder areas it may be better to lift them and heel them in in a sheltered part of your allotment.

from sowing to harvest
16 weeks.

where to plant
To crop well, parsnips need a deep, well-worked soil that is free from stones and in an open, sunny position.

soil preparation
Parsnips grow best in soil that was manured or composted for the previous crop. They benefit from the application of a low-fertility, organic mulch in winter before sowing.

sowing and planting
In milder areas sowing outside can begin in late winter, but as parsnip seed is slow to germinate it is better to leave sowing until mid-spring. Sow thinly in shallow drills or station sow at 3 seeds per station, thinning to 1 seedling per station. Early sowings can be made in small, biodegradable pots and planted out without disturbing the roots.

spacing
For small roots place seeds 10 cm (4 in) apart in drills that are 30 cm (12 in) apart. For larger roots sown in drills and in a bed system place seeds 15 cm (6 in) apart and drills or rows 30 cm (12 in) apart.

care
Keep the soil around seedlings weed-free until they are well established.

problems
Like carrots, carrot fly is the main problem when growing parsnips, and parsnip canker can sometimes occur, otherwise they are fairly trouble-free.

harvesting and storage
The flavour of parsnips improves after a frost. Lift the roots as required as the foliage begins to yellow. They can be left in the ground over winter, but older roots may develop a hard, woody core.

from sowing to harvest

16 to 36 weeks.

where to plant

As garlic is normally grown over winter, to thrive it needs a soil in an open position that does not become waterlogged in winter.

soil preparation

Soil that has been improved for a previous crop is ideal – don't plant in freshly manured soil.

sowing and planting

To grow the best sized bulbs most garlic is planted in autumn, as it needs a cold spell to grow well, but there are newer cultivars that can be planted in late winter or early spring. Divide the garlic in to individual cloves just before planting. Plant the cloves with the pointed end upward and the tip 2.5–10 cm (1–4 in) below soil level. If the soil is heavy clay plant the cloves shallowly.

spacing

Plant cloves 7.5–10 cm (3–4 in) apart in rows that are 24–30 cm (10–12 in) apart. In a bed system plant the cloves and the rows 18 cm (7 in) apart both ways.

care

Water in spring if the soil is dry and keep the area weed-free.

problems

Garlic is generally trouble free, but onion white rot, rust and downy mildew can be a problem.

harvesting and storage

Begin harvesting from mid- to late summer once the leaves begin to turn yellow. Dig up carefully and leave the bulbs to dry either in the open or in a cool, dry place. Lay the bulbs on a slatted shelf or hang up, and once dry tie into bunches. If stored correctly garlic will keep for up to 10 months.

Garlic (*Allium sativum*) is a vegetable that not everyone likes, but it is an easy crop. It is very hardy and needs a long growing season to crop well, but it takes up little space. It is grown from cloves – the individual segments of the bulb – and is never grown from seed. Buy garlic specifically for planting and not for eating as the latter may carry diseases. To grow well, garlic requires a cold period so it's best planted in autumn. Spring planted garlic may not mature well, especially in a poor summer.

Leeks

Leeks (*Allium porrum*) are a superb winter vegetable, beloved by the ordinary allotment gardener as well as by those who like to produce huge specimens for flower shows. Like all members of the onion family, they are easy to grow and undemanding. They don't take up much space and can be harvested over a long period from autumn to the following spring. The strong roots will also help to improve the structure of the soil. The edible part is the white stem, which is usually blanched by deep planting or by earthing up soil around the base of the plants.

from sowing to harvest

16 to 20 weeks.

where to plant

Leeks prefer a fertile soil that retains moisture in an open site – they will tolerate some shade.

soil preparation

Apply a high-fertility soil improver. If planted following a broad bean or pea crop apply a medium-fertility improver or a low-fertility improver with nitrogen-rich organic fertilizer.

sowing and planting

Seeds of leeks can be sown in early spring in pots indoors on the windowsill, but they can also be sown outdoors from early to mid-spring. For growing in the bed system sow seeds in modules with 5 or 6 seeds per cell in late winter or early spring. If sowing outside place the seeds in shallow drills 2.5 cm (1 in) deep, then transplant the seedlings to their final site. For both methods plant out when the seedlings are about 20 cm (8 in) tall, watering the plants well before transplanting in rows. Make a 15 cm (6 in) deep hole with a dibber and drop a single plant into each, then water in. The water will wash some soil into the hole.

spacing

Whether using traditional rows or a bed system space the plants in rows 15 x 23 cm (6 x 9 in) apart each way.

care

Water until the leek plants get established and if the soil is dry.

problems

Leek rust is the most common problem, otherwise they are relatively trouble-free.

harvesting and storage

Lift leeks as required as soon as they are large enough to use. Generally leeks are perfectly hardy, and will withstand most winter weather, so can be left in the ground until required.

from sowing to harvest

Spring sown seeds 20 to 24 weeks; autumn sown seeds 42 weeks; spring planted sets 18 to 20 weeks; and autumn planted sets 36 to 38 weeks.

where to plant

Most onions prefer an open, sunny site but will tolerate some shade. Autumn-sown seeds or planted sets need full sun and good drainage.

soil preparation

No organic matter need be applied if it was added for the previous crop. However, if this was not done apply a low- to medium-fertility soil improver, depending on the soil condition.

sowing and planting

Station sow seeds outside when the soil is warm enough, usually around mid-spring. Thin out to leave 1 seedling at each station. Plant onion sets from early to mid spring by pushing the sets into the soil, so the tips are just visible. For autumn-sown onion varieties sow seeds in late summer and thin out, as above. Plant autumn-sown onion sets in autumn. Summer varieties can be sown indoors in late winter.

spacing

Sow seeds 10 x 30 cm (4 x 12 in) apart each way. In a bed system sow 10 x 15 cm (4 x 6 in) apart each way.

care

Hand weed carefully as onions are shallow-rooted. In spring apply a nitrogen-rich organic fertilizer to over-wintered onions, if required.

problems

Onion fly, downy mildew, onion white rot and bolting (going to seed) are the main problems you may incur when growing onions.

harvesting and storage

Harvest when the bulbs are big enough to use. Dig up onions in dry weather and spread them out on slatted trays or on a raised bench for the skins to ripen. Once the skins are dry, hang up in a cool, frost-free place.

An allotment wouldn't be an allotment without a few rows of onions. Bulb or globe onions (*Allium cepa*) are a popular vegetable with those who grow for garden shows as well as with ordinary allotment-holders. You know you can always grow better onions than the next person! Fierce rivalries can build up in the run-up to a show, with tales of espionage and cheating all adding to the spice of the event. However, if you don't like the heat of competition you can still grow terrific onions. Here we will deal with bulb onions; for spring onions see page 91.

Shallots

Shallots (*Allium cepa* Aggregatum Group) are basically small onions, but they have a sweeter flavour. They are easier to grow and can be harvested earlier in summer. They are usually grown from sets, but can be grown from seed too, and form smaller shallots around the main bulb. Shallots require the same growing conditions as bulb onions and are ideal if space on the allotment is at a premium. There are yellow- and red-skinned cultivars, and you can eat them cooked or raw. The leaves can also be used in the same way as spring onions.

from sowing to harvest

20 weeks from seed; 20 to 24 weeks from sets.

where to plant

Shallots prefer an open, sunny site but they will tolerate some shade.

soil preparation

If organic matter was applied for a previous crop not organic matter need be applied. If not, apply low- to medium- fertility soil improve, depending on the soil condition.

sowing and planting

Shallots are mostly grown from sets and these are planted from late winter to mid-spring. Plant the sets by taking out a hole with a trowel or take out a drill. The tip of the set should be at soil level. Sow seeds in early and mid-spring in drills and thin out.

spacing

Space shallot sets, or thin seedlings, so they are 15 cm (6 in) apart in rows 30 cm (12 in) apart. If you are using a bed system reduce the spacing to 15 cm (6 in) apart each way.

care

Little attention is needed to care for shallots other than to water the plants in dry weather, particularly as the bulbs begin to swell.

problems

The problems that affect onions can also affect shallots (see page 87), but generally they are trouble-free.

harvesting and storage

Lift shallots when the leaves begin to die back, usually around midsummer onward, and leave them lying on the surface of the soil to dry. Once the skins are dry, store in a cool, frost-free place in nets or in single layers on slated trays.

from sowing to harvest

8 weeks.

where to plant

An open site is preferred to grow well, but they will tolerate a little shade.

soil preparation

No organic matter need be applied if it was done for a previous crop. If not, apply a low- to medium-fertility soil improver, depending on the soil. Shallots will tolerate poorer soil conditions than other onions.

sowing and planting

This type of onion can be sown in modules indoors, 5 or 6 seeds per cell, in late winter or early spring, and planted out when about 10 cm (4 in) tall. Don't thin out. Outside sow from spring to summer every 3 weeks for a continuous supply of spring onions. For a spring crop sow suitable cultivars in late summer. This is a useful way of growing them in bands.

spacing

Sow seeds thinly in rows 10 cm (4 in) apart, or if you want a lot of spring onions at the same time, in bands up to 15 cm (6 in) wide. Aim to place seeds about 1–2.5cm (½–1 in) apart.

care

Water well in dry conditions and protect winter crops with cloches in severe weather.

problems

Spring onions are susceptible to the same problems as other onions, but generally are trouble free.

harvesting and storage

Harvest by pulling them from the soil when they are about 15 cm (6 in) high. Spring onions will keep for a few days in the refrigerator, but are best eaten fresh from the garden.

Spring or salad onions (*Allium cepa*) are smaller than other onions and have a milder flavour. They don't store well and are best eaten fresh. Traditionally used in salads and for flavouring other dishes, they are easy to grow. They grow quickly and are usually ready to harvest about 8 weeks after sowing. Germination can be a little erratic at times, and multi sowing in modules is a good way to start them off. Place the modular tray in a sheltered place outdoors or in a shady cold frame and they'll germinate well. In most areas they will overwinter if covered with cloches or horticultural fleece.

Sweetcorn

While not part of the onion family, sweetcorn has been included here, as it requires similar soil conditions to onions, and it is the only plant from the *Poaceae* family included in the vegetable directory. Home-grown sweetcorn (*Zea mays*), which is eaten as soon as it has been cut, tastes far better than anything you can buy – if you leave it for any length of time the sugar turns to starch. It is a wind-pollinated crop that needs plenty of sun, so it is best to plant it in blocks rather than in rows. Although it's easy to grow, it tends to be less successful in cooler summers.

from sowing to harvest
10 to 15 weeks.

where to plant
A warm, sheltered, sunny spot with well-drained soil is the best location for sweetcorn. Avoid very dry or very heavy clay soils.

soil preparation
Sweetcorn grows best in soil that has been manured or composted for a previous crop. If not done before planting, apply a medium-fertility soil improver.

sowing and planting
Sweetcorn needs a mimimum temperature of 10°C (50°F) to germinate. In colder areas sow seeds indoors in 8 cm² (3 in²) modules or biodegradable pots with 1 seed per pot. Harden off before planting out when the threat of frost has passed. Planting through black polythene, which warms the soil, will speed up growth and increase the quantity of cobs you harvest.

spacing
Plant in blocks rather than rows with 35 cm (14 in) between the plants each way – for mini cobs leave 15 cm (6 in) between the plants. Supersweet cultivars are best grown at least 8 m (25 ft) from other varieties to prevent cross pollination.

care
As the plants are tall they may need support on exposed sites – earth up the soil around the base of the stems for extra support. In dry conditions water when the corn starts to swell, hand-weed or mulch to keep down weeds and retain moisture in the soil.

problems
Slugs, mice and birds can be a problem.

harvesting and storage
The corn is ripe when the tassels at the top of each cob turn brown – press a thumbnail into a corn grain and a milky juice should appear.

from sowing to harvest

12 weeks.

where to plant

Grow in a warm, sheltered site in moisture-retentive soil. Cucumbers grow best with a minimum temperature of 18°C (64°F).

soil preparation

Apply a low- to medium-fertility soil improver before planting. On heavy soils mound up soil before planting to improve drainage.

sowing and planting

Cucumbers are best sown under cover in a heated propagator with a minimum temperature of 20°C (68°F). Seedlings will need a minimum temperature of 16°C (60°F) to grow well. Sow seeds in modules or biodegradable pots with 1 seed per module cell or pot. Grow on and plant out when the threat of frost has passed. In colder areas young plants may need the protection of cloches until they become established.

spacing

Grow in rows 45–100 cm (18–39 in). In the bed system plant 75 cm (30 in) apart each way.

care

Trailing types are best grown up canes or similar supports; pinch out the growing tips of the plants when they reach the tops of the supports to encourage sideshoots and more fruits to form. Ridge types can be grown on the flat. Pinch out the growing tips when they have produced 5 or 6 leaves. Water regularly through the season and mulch with straw to keep the fruits of ridge types clean.

problems

Slugs and aphids can be a problem.

harvesting and storage

Cut the fruits when they are large enough to use. Use fresh from the plants or keep in a fridge for 3 or 4 days.

Cucumbers (*Cucumis sativus*) have a trailing habit, and plants can grow to 3 m (10 ft) long. New introductions have made it possible to grow them outside perfectly well in many areas. So-called ridge cucumbers are distinctive in that they have rough skins. It was the practice in the past to grow cucumbers on specially prepared ridges of soil, but modern cultivars do not need this treatment. A wigwam of canes is a good way to support them: this way they take up less space on the allotment, other crops can be grown around them, and the fruits are not spoiled by soil splashes when it rains.

Courgettes and marrows

Courgettes (*Cucurbita pepo*) are actually immature marrows, and you grow them in exactly the same way. Some cultivars have a trailing habit, while others are more compact and bushy. Choose the bushy ones, which take up less space, for an allotment. The skin of the fruits can be green, yellow or striped. You can eat the flowers, raw or cooked, and the young leaves and shoots as well as the fruits. To get the best from them, start them off indoors, but you can start them outside in milder regions. They are easy to grow and very rewarding.

from sowing to harvest

Courgettes 6 weeks after planting out; marrows from 7 to 8 weeks.

where to plant

Marrows prefer a sheltered site in full sun. Courgettes can be grown under cloches for an earlier crop.

soil preparation

Too rich a soil will promote a lot of leaf growth at the expense of fruits. Apply a low- or medium-fertility soil improver depending on the condition of the soil.

sowing and planting

Sow seeds in late spring, 3 or 4 weeks before the last frosts are expected. Sow 1 seed per 8 cm (3 in) pot in a warm place and harden off before planting out.

spacing

Compact, bushy cultivars take up less space so can be planted 60–90 x 90–120 (24–36 x 36–48 in) apart. Plant trailing cultivars 1.2–1.8 m x 1.8 m (4–6 ft x 6ft) apart. If using the bed system, allow 90 cm (36 in) each way for bush plants and 1.2 m–1.8 m (4–6 ft) for trailing plants.

care

Keep the soil weed free and water only until the plants become established. Trailing cultivars can be trained up supports so they take up less space.

problems

Slugs can be a problem particularly with young plants; powdery mildew can also be problematic.

harvesting and storage

Pick courgettes when they are around 10–15 cm (4–6 in) long; the more you pick the more you will get. For storage, leave marrows on the plants for as long as possible. From early autumn pick marrows when they are hard and sound hollow if tapped with your finger. Well-ripened marrows can be kept for up to 12 months in a cool, airy, frost-free place. Courgettes will keep in the fridge for up to 3 weeks.

from sowing to harvest
12 to 20 weeks.

where to plant
Melons can be grown under cloches or in a cold frame. Newer cultivars are suitable for growing outdoors without protection.

soil preparation
Apply a medium-fertility or low-fertility soil improver and an organic fertilizer, if necessary.

sowing and planting
Sow seeds, 1 per 8 cm (3 in) pot, at a temperature of 18°C (64°F) from mid- to late spring. Seeds germinate better if sown on their edge. Grow on at a minimum temperature of 13°C (55°F) and plant out when the threat of frost has passed. If plants become pot-bound pot in to 13 cm (5 in) pots to keep them growing.

spacing
For plants grown on the ground and allowed to trail allow 1 x 1–1.6 m (3 x 3–5 ft). For those trained up supports, allow 38 cm (15 in) for single cordons and 60 cm (24 in) for double cordons. In the bed system, use the same spacings.

care
Protect young plants from the cold with cloches. Once flowers are showing, remove the cloches to allow insects to pollinate the flowers. Water plants regularly. Plants grown on the flat can be left to trail, but after 5 leaves have formed pinch out the growing tip and allow 4 sideshoots to grow. With trained plants allow 1 or 2 shoots for each plant and pinch out the growing tips when the plants are 2 m (6 ft) high. Continue tying in subsequent growths and pinch out the tips when 5 leaves have formed. Allow 4 to 5 fruits per plant.

problems
Aphids and mildew can be troublesome.

harvesting and storage
Melons are ready to eat from late summer onward. Ripe melons smell sweet.

Sweet melons (*Cucumis melo*), which are annuals, are normally trained as cordons (single stems), and the main types are cantaloupe, winter (or casaba) and musk. They are tropical plants and require warm temperatures to grow well. However, newer cultivars make it possible to grow them under cloches in cooler climates and some can be grown outside without any protection. Melons are worth growing, for there is nothing like the taste of a fresh melon taken straight from the plant on a warm day.

Pumpkins and squashes

Pumpkins (*Cucurbita maxima*, *C. moschata*, *C. pepo*) are quite a novelty to grow. However, since they grow quickly and the results can be spectacular, they are great for getting children interested in gardening and growing food. There are many secrets and tales swapped among allotment-holders about the best way to grow pumpkins. Only some, such as urinating on the plants, are repeatable. The sizes and shapes of the fruits vary considerably. While it is the giant pumpkins that most people are tempted to try, the smaller-fruited cultivars are far better for eating. You can grow the smaller fruited squashes up a strong wigwam support, but leave the giants to trail on the ground.

from sowing to harvest

Summer squashes 7–8 weeks after planting out; pumpkins up to 20 weeks after planting out.

where to plant

Plant in a sheltered site in full sun. Small fruiting kinds can be trained up supports.

soil preparation

Apply a low- or medium-fertility soil improver, depending on the soil type. A soil that is too rich encourages a lot of leaf growth.

sowing and planting

Pumpkins and squashes need a minimum temperature of 13°C (55°F). Sow in late spring, putting 1 seed in each 8 cm (3 in) pot. Harden off before planting when the threat of frost has passed. Seeds can be sown directly outside in early summer in milder areas.

spacing

With bush cultivars, plant 60–90 x 90–120 cm (24–36 x 36–48 in) apart. For trailing cultivars, plant 1.2–1.8 x 1.8 m (4–6 x 6 ft) apart and in the bed system allow 1 m (36 in) for bush plants and 1.2–1.8 m (4–6 ft) for trailing plants.

care

Trailing cultivars of summer squashes can be trained up supports. Keep the soil around the plants weed-free and water only until the plants become established. With larger pumpkins only keep 3 to 4 fruits per plant.

problems

Look our for slugs, particularly in young plants, and in cold wet weather powdery mildew can be troublesome.

harvesting and storing

Harvest summer squashes when they are large enough to eat, and keep in the fridge for up to 3 weeks. Fruits are ready to harvest when they are hard and sound hollow when tapped. Well-ripened fruits will store for up to 12 months in a cool, airy, frost-free place.

from sowing to harvest

Spring-sown up to 16 weeks; autumn-sown up to 35 weeks.

where to plant

Broad beans prefer an open, sunny site. Winter crops may need some shelter: protect with cloches in colder areas. Broad beans do not grow well on either dry or waterlogged soil. They are tolerant of some lime or slightly alkaline soils.

soil preparation

Apply a low-fertility soil improver to light, sandy soils before sowing seeds.

sowing and planting

For early crops, sow indoors in modules or biodegradable pots with 1 seed per cell or pot from late winter to early spring. Plant out under cloches when 3 or 4 true leaves have formed. Outside, sow from early to late spring, and in autumn for a crop the following year.

spacing

If sowing in rows, seeds are usually sown in double rows, 15–20 cm (6–8 in) between the seeds and 60 cm (24 in) between each double row, with seeds sown 5 cm (2 in) deep. In the bed system sow or plant 20–30 cm (8–12 in) apart each way.

care

Pinch out the growing tips of plants when the flowers begin to open; this deters aphids and encourages pods to form. Support tall cultivars with canes and string.

problems

Mice can dig up seeds and eat seedlings, and pigeons can also eat young plants. Aphids and broad bean chocolate spot can also be troublesome.

harvesting and storage

Harvest the pods when the beans can be felt through the skins, before the beans become tough to eat.

Broad beans (*Vicia faba*), also known as fava beans, are a fantastic vegetable to grow and wonderful value. You can sow in autumn for an early crop, and make another sowing in spring. They are a useful green manure crop, because the plants return nitrogen to the soil. Most will need staking, but there are a number of dwarf cultivars that do not. If you enjoy these beans raw, harvest them while they are young, because left too long the flavour deteriorates and the beans become hard. The young shoot tips are also edible.

Broad beans

French beans

There are dwarf and climbing French beans (*Phaseolus vulgaris*), which makes them a versatile crop and one that can be grown in a small space. Climbing French beans will need support, like runner beans (see opposite) and they crop over a long period. The pods can be round, flat or curved in shape and up to 20 cm (8 in) long. They may be green, yellow, purple or red in colour. They require similar growing conditions to runner beans and grow best in a rich, moisture-retentive but well-drained soil.

from sowing to harvest

7 to 18 weeks depending on cultivar.

where to plant

They prefer a warm, sheltered site and warm soil.

soil preparation

On reasonable soil no additional preparation is needed, particularly if it has been prepared well for a previous crop. Otherwise, add a medium-fertility soil improver before sowing or planting.

sowing and planting

To get an early crop, start off in pots or modules from early to mid-spring. Harden off before planting out when the threat of frost has passed. Outside, begin sowing from early to late summer. Covering the soil with polythene or cloches 2 or 3 weeks before sowing will warm the soil. Sow seeds 5 cm (2 in) deep.

spacing

Plant dwarf cultivars in rows 5 x 45 cm (2 x 18 in) apart. Climbing cultivars are best grown up wigwams or in double rows, 60 cm (24 in) apart, with 1.5 m (5 ft) between rows and 15 cm (6 in) between supports. If you are using the bed system, sow or plant 15–20 cm (6–8 in) apart each way. Dwarf cultivars are best for the bed system.

care

Use tall canes or similar to support climbing cultivars. Seeds and seedlings can be protected with bottle cloches to prevent pests eating the seeds. Watering when the pods begin to develop can increase the crop.

problems

Mice, aphids and viruses can be troublesome.

harvesting and storage

Pick as soon as they are large enough, that is, when they are about 10 cm (4 in) long and they snap easily, before the seeds are visible inside. Check plants almost daily as the beans develop quickly. If you want to dry the beans, do not pick any pods fresh but leave them on the plant until they turn brown.

from sowing to harvest

12 to 16 weeks.

where to plant

A sheltered, sunny site with moisture-retentive soil is preferable.

soil preparation

Grow in soil that has had soil improvers applied for a previous crop. If necessary, apply a low-fertility soil improver to help retain moisture in the soil.

sowing and planting

Seeds can be sown indoors in mid-spring to plant out in late spring or early summer when the threat of frost has passed. Sow seeds in biodegradable pots or modular trays with one seeds per pot or tray cell and place on the windowsill. In milder areas seeds can be sown outside from late spring to early summer. Station sow 2 seeds per station.

spacing

In conventional rows, plants are usually grown in double rows 15 x 60 cm (6 x 24 in) or 15–30 cm (6–12 in) apart if grown as wigwams. If you are using the bed system, plant dwarf cultivars only 30 cm (12 in) apart each way.

care

The plants are heavy when fully grown and need substantial supports from 2.5 m (8 ft) bamboo canes or bean poles, if you can get them. Mulch the plants when established to help retain moisture and water regularly in dry weather when the first flower buds appear. The flowers need pollinating to produce pods.

problems

Slugs are the main pest of beans. A poor pod set can be due to cold weather resulting in few pollinating insects being around, or a shortage of water in the soil.

harvesting and storage

Pick pods when they are around 15 cm (6 in) long; picking regularly encourages more pods to form.

Runner beans (*Phaseolus coccineus*) are one of the most popular vegetables grown on allotments. Because the flowers and foliage are attractive you can grow them in the garden as well. Grow them mixed with sweet peas for a really attractive feature. Dwarf cultivars will need some support in the form of canes or bean poles. There are many ways of providing support, including making wigwams or erecting rows of stakes or training plants up strings attached to a horizontal piece of wood supported on stakes. Use whichever method is best for you and your available space.

It is impossible to beat the flavour of fresh peas (*Pisum sativum*) picked from the plant. In fact, you might find that you eat them all before you have time to get them near the kitchen. If you choose cultivars carefully you can have peas for most of the summer. They are easy to grow and require little effort. Taller cultivars will need fairly substantial support, and even dwarf cultivars will benefit from having a few twiggy sticks around them. It can be a good idea to cover the seeds after sowing with horticultural fleece to keep mice and pigeons at bay.

from sowing to harvest

For early cultivars, 11 to 12 weeks and maincrop cultivars, 13 to 14 weeks.

where to plant

Peas prefer soil that does not dry out in summer, but is not waterlogged in winter.

soil preparation

Apply a low-fertility soil improver if the soil has not been improved for a previous crop.

sowing and planting

Use early cultivars for early and late sowings. The earliest crops can be started of in pots or modules from late winter onwards. Harden off and transplant when plants are 10 cm (4 in) tall, planting under cloches in colder areas. Outside, begin sowing in mid-spring and continue at regular intervals until midsummer.

spacing

Outside sow in 10–15 cm (4–6 in) wide drills. Scatter the seeds in the bottom of the drills so they are around 5 cm (2 in) apart. Leave 60 cm–1 m (24–36 in) between the drills, depending on the height of each cultivar.

care

Put supports in place early before the plants begin to fall over; stem tendrils will cling to any supports provided. Leafless and semi-leafless cultivars are self-supporting, requiring little extra support if grown in a block. Water regularly in dry conditions from when the first flowers open.

problems

Pigeons love to eat the young plants and mice will also take the seeds. Pea moth can be troublesome too.

harvesting and storage

Check the plants regularly and harvest peas when the pods are plump, but not too large. Mangetout cultivars are picked as soon as the pods are large enough to use, before peas start to form.

from sowing to harvest

Varies depending on cultivar.

where to plant

Chicory will tolerate some shade, but avoid light sandy or heavy clay soils. Winter-forcing types need a good, deep soil to enable them to produce good roots for forcing. The non-forcing types can be grown under cloches to extend the season.

soil preparation

No special preparation is needed if the soil has been improved for a previous crop. If not, apply a medium-fertility soil improver before sowing or planting.

sowing and planting

Cultivars that are to be forced are sown from early to late summer whereas salad types are sown from mid-spring to late summer, outside.

spacing

Forcing cultivars are spaced 20 x 30 cm (8 x 12 in) and salad cultivars 20–35 cm (8–14 in). In the bed system spacing is 20 x 30 cm (8 x 12 in)

care

Give plants plenty of water until they are established. Cover with fleece or cloches if frost is forecast. Dig up roots of forcing cultivars from late autumn onward.

problems

Slugs can be a problem, but otherwise chicory is relatively trouble-free.

harvesting and storage

With forced chicory grown in pots, harvest when the chicons are about 10–13 cm (4–5 in) tall. To force chicory, dig up roots in autumn through winter and pot up 3 or 4 roots in 23 cm (9 in) pots and cover with the same size pot, making sure to cover any drainage holes to exclude light. Keep the pots in a frost-free place and harvest as for salad cultivars. With salad cultivars, pick individual leaves, cut the whole plant or leave the stumps, which will regrow.

There are two types of chicory (*Cichorium intybus*): one that needs blanching and is harvested in winter and spring, and one that does not need blanching and is eaten like lettuce. Blanched chicory is one of the finest winter vegetables, with a slightly bitter yet refreshing taste. The summer and autumn salad types come in a wide range of colours, adding vibrant shades to any salad. The winter-blanching types need to be grown through the summer to build up enough reserves in the large taproots for winter forcing.

Globe artichokes

Globe artichokes (*Cynara scolymus*) are striking architectural plants that do not look out of place grown in an ornamental border, and are a delicious vegetable, too, although they do take up a lot of space. Easier to grow than many people think, they can be grown as annuals or perennials. The green and purple flower buds are the edible part, and they are cooked or pickled. Once the flowers open they become inedible, but the great thistle-like flowers are great for attracting bees and other pollinating insects to your allotment.

from sowing to harvest

Around 28 weeks from planting in a plant's first season and subsequently in late spring and early summer.

where to plant

Globe artichokes prefer a sheltered site, avoiding wet or heavy clay soils.

soil preparation

On dry soils, apply a high-fertility soil improver.

sowing and planting

Sow seeds in late winter or early spring. New plants can also be grown from offsets or divisions from established plants in spring.

spacing

Globe artichokes need a lot of space: at least 1–1.5 m (3 x 5 ft) for each plant. In deep beds allow 45 cm (18 in) each way between the plants and grow them as annuals.

care

Water the plants until they become established and mulch with hay or compost. The best crop is obtained from plants until they are 3–4 years old so take offsets from plants every 2 or 3 years.

problems

Artichokes are usually trouble-free, but aphids can be troublesome.

harvesting and storage

Harvest artichokes when the buds are still tight and eat fresh from July to September. Cook the buds whole and eat the fleshy parts at the base of the scales. The heart at the top of the stem can be eaten after removing the fibrous 'choke'.

from sowing to harvest

16 to 20 weeks.

where to plant

Jerusalem artichokes will grow in sun or part shade, but avoid poorly drained soils.

soil preparation

If the soil has not been improved for previous crops apply a medium-fertility soil improver before planting the tubers. Using a higher fertility improver will give larger tubers to harvest.

sowing and planting

The tubers are usually planted in late winter or early spring, around 15 cm (6 in) deep.

spacing

Space rows at 30 cm x 1 m (12 in x 3 ft), and in the bed system 45 cm (18 in) apart each way.

care

Some support with stout posts may be needed. Water during dry spells and remove flower buds to increase the yield. Cut down top growth when it turns brown.

problems

Jerusalem artichokes are usually trouble-free, but can occasionally be attacked by slugs and wireworms.

harvesting and storage

Tubers are best used soon after harvesting as they do not keep for long – dig up and use as required from late autumn onward. Some tubers can be kept for replanting for the following season. If you want to clear the area, make sure you remove all tubers as they will regrow like potatoes.

Jerusalem artichokes (*Helianthus tuberosus*) are grown for the roots, which resemble potatoes. They have a similar flavour to globe artichokes (see opposite) but are easier to grow. The plants can be invasive if they are not kept in check. Try growing them on their own at one end of the allotment, where the plants, which can grow to 3 m (10 ft) or more, act as a good windbreak. The plants can also be used to screen your shed or compost heap from view. Jerusalem artichokes tolerate a wide range of soil types, and you can eat the tubers raw or cooked.

Lettuce (*Latuca sativa*) is the mainstay of summer salads, but in the last few years it has undergone little short of a revolution. We no longer have just the plain-leaved, green kind, but a choice of frilly-leaved ones, hearted or loose-leaf types, cut-and-come-again cultivars and all in different colours. Choosing the right cultivars can give you lettuces almost all year round. Because they grow fairly quickly, lettuces are ideal as a catch crop or for intercropping between rows of slower maturing crops, such as winter brassicas. Sow at 14-day intervals through the season for a succession, and to avoid having a glut at any one time.

from sowing to harvest
4 to 14 weeks.

where to plant
Lettuce will grow in most soils except poorly drained or very dry soils. Intercrop lettuces between rows of longer-term crops such as brassicas. They prefer sun, but will tolerate part shade.

soil preparation
No special soil preparation is needed where soil has been improved for previous crops. On poor soils, a medium-fertility soil improver will benefit lettuces.

sowing and planting
Start sowing summer cultivars indoors in gentle heat from late winter onward and sow seeds at 14-day intervals for a succession of lettuces. Outside, begin sowing from mid-spring onward at regular intervals until early autumn. Sow in shallow drills 15 cm (6 in) apart and thin seedlings, when large enough to handle, to the same distance. When sown as above, lettuces can be used as a cut-and-come-again crop (cut to about 2 cm (¾ in) and left to grow again). They can also be sown broadcast – when they are not thinned.

spacing
This varies depending on the cultivar. Grown in rows, space 15–30 x 20–34 cm (6–12 x 8–14 in) apart, and in the bed system, 15–30 cm (6–12 in) each way.

care
Water plants until they are established and during dry spells. Keep free of weeds.

problems
Slugs, aphids, botrytis and downy mildew.

harvesting and storage
With hearted cultivars, harvest as soon as the hearts are firm; with loose-leaf cultivars pick leaves from the outside of the plants as required. With seedling crops, cut when the young plants are about 5 cm (2 in) tall, usually around 4 weeks after sowing. Three or four such harvests can be taken.

from sowing to harvest

8 to 12 months.

where to plant

An open site, but protected from cold winds, is preferable, with good, fertile soil.

soil preparation

Before planting, apply a medium-fertility soil improver or plant after a nitrogen-fixing green manure.

sowing and planting

Seeds can be sown indoors in modules in early spring or sown in seed beds outdoors from mid- to late spring. Sow in shallow drills 2–2.5 cm (¾–1 in) deep. Transplant seedlings from early to midsummer when they have made 2 or 3 true leaves (which are distinct from the seed leaves which emerge first). Plant out indoor grown plants 4–5 weeks after sowing, and harden off before planting.

spacing

Space plants out 60 cm (24 in) apart in the rows and allow 75 cm (30 in) between the rows. In the bed system, space plants 60 cm (24 in) each way.

care

Protect young plants from birds with netting or fleece, and water until the plants become established. Later, the plants may need staking.

problems

Cabbage root fly, aphids, cabbage white butterflies and flea beetles can all be troublesome.

harvesting and storage

Snap off the florets as they show, but before the buds begin to open. Regular harvesting of the florets will encourage more shoots to grow. Harvesting can go on for up to 2 months.

Easy-to-grow sprouting broccoli (*Brassica oleracea* Italica Group) is grown for the individual florets, which are similar to, though smaller than, cauliflowers. There are white and purple forms, and the purple forms are hardier than the white ones. It is the flowering shoots, which develop in spring, that are eaten. Broccoli is regarded as a hardy vegetable, which can be grown in almost any conditions. It is a slow-growing crop and requires a good, fertile soil. Because it takes up a lot of space, grow crops such as lettuce and radishes as intercrops between the rows of broccoli.

Some people find Brussels sprouts (*Brassica oleracea* Gemmifera Group) an acquired taste, but they are an invaluable winter crop. Modern F1 hybrids are a great improvement on older cultivars because some are dwarf and so take up less space. Given that they take up quite a lot of space, consider growing quick-maturing crops, such as lettuce, radishes and spring onions, between them. You can eat the tops as well as the sprouts, making them good value for money. Choose cultivars that crop over a long period to have sprouts from late autumn to late winter.

from sowing to harvest

Around 20 weeks.

where to plant

The best crop will be produced in an open site in full sun, with firm soil.

soil preparation

Brussels sprouts are gross feeders so apply a medium-fertility soil improver with a general organic fertilizer before planting in spring, or grow in soil which has had a nitrogen-fixing green manure growing in it beforehand. If the plants are not growing well, apply a nitrogen-rich fertilizer such as pelleted chicken manure in midsummer.

sowing and planting

For early crops, sow seeds in trays or modules indoors in early spring. Before planting out, harden off and plant out around 6 weeks after sowing. Outside sow from early to mid-spring depending on your area. Sow seeds thinly in short rows 15 cm (6 in) apart. Transplant seedlings from late spring to early summer.

spacing

In rows, space dwarf cultivars 45 cm (18 in) apart and tall cultivars 60 cm (24 in) apart each way. In the bed system space 45–75 cm (18–30 in) apart each way, depending on cultivar.

care

On windy, exposed sites you may have to stake the taller cultivars as they grow; earthing-up stems can also provide a little support. Remove any yellowing leaves and keep the plants weed-free.

problems

Flea beetle, cabbage root fly, cabbage white butterfly, white fly and pigeons are common problems.

harvesting and storage

Leave until the first frost as sprouts taste better after being frosted. Start harvesting from the bottom of the plants, taking a few from each plant.

from sowing to harvest

Around 20 weeks.

where to plant

An open, sunny site is good and cabbages will tolerate exposed sites.

soil preparation

Like other brassicas cabbages are gross feeders so apply a medium-fertility soil improver, or a low-fertility soil improver plus a general organic fertilizer before planting. Or grow in soil which has had a nitrogen-fixing green manure growing in it the previous year.

sowing and planting

Sow summer and autumn cultivars from late winter indoors and early to late spring outside. Plant out the earliest sowings under cloches or when the soil is workable. Outside, sow autumn and winter cultivars in late spring. Spring cabbages are sown in autumn. Sow in seedbeds in short rows 15 cm (6 in) apart

spacing

Spacing of plants varies depending on the cultivars grown but generally 30–45 cm (12–18 in) each way is adequate for summer and autumn types. For winter types plant around 45 cm (18 in) apart, for spring cabbages plant 15 cm (6 in) apart and harvest every other one to leave them 30 cm (12 in) apart.

care

Protect seedlings and young plants from pigeons and flea beetle and cabbage root fly. Water young plants until they are established.

problems

Cabbage root fly, caterpillars, flea beetles and clubroot are the main problems that affect cabbages.

harvesting and storage

Cut all cabbages as needed. Spring cabbages can give a second crop of greens if you cut a cross in the stalks left in the ground: new shoots soon begin to sprout. Autumn and winter cabbages can be stored in a cool frost-free place, cover with straw, sacks or newspapers.

If you choose the right varieties it is possible to harvest cabbage (*Brassica oleracea* Capitata Group) throughout the year. Sadly it is another vegetable that is often cooked to death, but cabbages can be invaluable, particularly through the winter, when little else is available. You can eat the leaves raw, but most people prefer to cook them. Cabbages are divided into spring, summer and autumn-winter types. They are a rewarding crop, and the summer types in particular are fairly quick to grow.

Calabrese (*Brassica oleracea* Italica Group) is often referred to as broccoli in the green grocers. Rather than produce lots of sideshoots with spears or small heads on them, as sprouting broccoli does, calabrese tends to produce fewer heads, but once the main one is harvested plants will generally produce new shoots to harvest. It is another hardy vegetable and can be grown in any area, although hard frosts may damage young, embryonic heads as they develop. It is a fast-maturing crop and is easy to grow. It is normally eaten lightly cooked.

from sowing to harvest
11 to 14 weeks.

where to plant
Open, but protected from cold winds. It can be cropped early or late under cover.

soil preparation
If soil is poor, apply a medium-fertility soil improver or a low-fertility soil improver along with a general organic fertilizer. Alternatively, plant after a nitrogen-fixing green manure.

sowing and planting
Sow seeds in biodegradable modules or pots as this brasicca resents root disturbance. For early crops, sow in spring. Outside station sow 2 or 3 seeds per station. Thin out to leave the strongest seedling. Plant out indoor-raised plants when the threat of frost has passed or plant under cloches for protection from frost.

spacing
Plant in rows spaced at 60 cm (24 in) apart each way and in the bed system space at 45 cm (18 in) apart.

care
Protect young plants from birds and keep watered until they become established and during dry spells. Mulch with compost after harvesting the central head to encourage more sideshoots to form. To keep pests such as cabbage white butterflies at bay cover the plants with environmesh or fleece.

problems
Cabbage root fly, aphids, caterpillars, birds and flea beetles are the main problems to affect calabrese.

harvesting and storage
Cut the central head while the buds are still tight. Two or three more pickings can be had from sideshoots.

from sowing to harvest

16 to 40 weeks, depending on the cultivar.

where to plant

An open, sunny site in a fertile, moisture-retentive soil.

soil preparation

As cauliflowers are gross feeders apply a medium-fertility soil improver before planting or a low-fertility improver with a general organic fertilizer. Alternatively, follow on from a nitrogen-fixing green manure crop.

sowing and planting

Cauliflowers are best sown in biodegradable pots or modules to minimize root disturbance, which will check the plants' growth. For early summer crops sow indoors from mid-autumn to late winter; for late summer crops sow indoors in early spring; for an autumn harvest sow outdoors in mid-spring; and for a winter crops sow in late spring.

spacing

In traditional rows space plants 45 cm (18 in) apart in rows that are 60 cm (24 in) apart. Space mini cultivars 10 cm (4 in) apart in rows that are spaced 23 cm (9 in) apart. If using a bed system space the plants 30 cm (12 in) apart each way.

care

To grow cauliflowers well keep them watered in dry weather and mulch to retain moisture in the soil. Tie up leaves to protect the curd (the edible flower head) in winter.

problems

Clubroot, cabbage rootfly, cabbage white butterflies and pigeons are the main problems that affect cauliflowers.

harvesting and storage

Select small, white curds while the florets are still tight – once the curds begin to turn yellowish it's a sign they are overmature. Cauliflowers can be kept in the fridge for about a week or you can hang them upside down in a cool, airy place for up to 3 weeks.

Cauliflower (*Brassica oleracea* Botrytis Group) is another brassica that attracts mixed emotions: people either love it or hate it. Some people think that cauliflowers have little flavour and that, as with Brussels sprouts, they turn soggy when cooked for too long. They can be difficult to grow well and they need plenty of moisture, and for this reason, the autumn- and spring-heading types are far easier to grow. Because cauliflowers are large plants and remain in the ground for up to a year, if yours is a compact plot try early-summer and mini varieties.

Although it is not the tastiest of vegetables, kale (*Brassica oleracea* Acephala Group) is highly nutritious and full of vitamins. It is sometimes known as borecole, which is a Dutch word meaning peasants' cabbage. Kale is reliably hardy and useful in cold winters, and there are newer varieties that are an improvement on older ones and that are well worth trying. Dwarf cultivars are available if space is tight or your allotment is on an exposed site. Kale is a good standby when there is little else to eat from the allotment.

from sowing to harvest

From 7 weeks (see below, harvesting and storage).

where to plant

Kale will tolerate poorer soils better than other brassicas. It will also tolerate some shade, but will not tolerate poorly drained soils.

soil preparation

Improve soil, if necessary, by applying a medium-fertility soil improver or a low-fertility soil improver with a general organic fertilizer. Alternatively, follow on from a nitrogen-fixing green manure. If the soil is too rich the resulting growth may be too lush and it will not withstand frosty weather.

sowing and planting

For a summer crop sow seeds indoors in late winter in modules or trays. Outside sow in drills in mid- to late spring and transplant seedlings 6–8 weeks later. Sow in a seedbed in shallow drills 15 cm (6 in) apart in early spring for summer crops and in late spring for autumn and winter crops.

spacing

Dwarf cultivars can be planted as close as 30 cm (12 in) apart, but taller cultivars are better spaced at 60–75 cm (24–30 in).

care

Water seedlings until they are established and keep the bed plants weed-free throughout the season.

problems

Cabbage white butterfly, aphids, white fly, pigeons and clubroot are the main problems affecting kale.

harvesting and storage

Pick 10–12.5 cm (4–5 in) long leaves as required from mature plants or remove a few smaller leaves at a time from younger plants for a quicker harvest. For some cultivars harvesting can start as soon as 7 weeks after sowing, but the plants will stand for a long time giving a longer harvesting period. Kale is often more flavoursome after a frost.

from sowing to harvest

Summer cultivars 4 weeks; mooli cultivars 7 to 8 weeks; and autumn and winter cultivars around 20 weeks.

where to plant

Radishes will grow in an open site, but they benefit from some shade from other crops in summer. This makes them an ideal crop for inter-cropping between any slower maturing crops.

soil preparation

Radishes prefer soil that has been improved for a previous crop. Otherwise, simply apply a low-fertility soil improver.

sowing and planting

Radishes don't transplant, but they can be multi-sown in modules (5 or 6 seeds per cell) and planted out without disturbing the roots. For early crops, sow indoors from late winter to early spring. Sow outside from spring to autumn at 10-day intervals. Mooli cultivars are sown in late summer and winter cultivars from mid to late summer.

spacing

Sow summer cultivars in rows 10 cm (4 in) apart and thin to 2.5 cm (1 in) apart. Alternatively, sow in broad bands 10–15 cm (4–6 in) wide in the bed system and thin to 2.5 cm (1 in) apart. Sow mooli and winter cultivars in traditional rows or a bed system 10 cm (4 in) apart in rows that are 25 cm (10 in) apart.

care

Do not allow the plants to dry out, but don't over-water either as this can encourage a lot of leafy growth

problems

Flea beetles can be a problem, but otherwise radishes are relatively trouble-free as they grow so quickly.

harvesting and storage

Harvest summer and mooli cultivars as soon as they are large enough to use and winter cultivars from autumn to spring – protect them with straw or braken in bad weather.

Radishes (*Raphanus sativus, R. sativus* Longipinnatus Group) are one of the easiest of all vegetables to grow, and because they grow so quickly they are ideal for introducing children to the joys of gardening and growing their own food. Grow radishes as a catch crop between other slower maturing crops. They will tolerate a wide range of soil conditions, although in summer they will benefit from a bit of shade from other crops. The range of varieties has increased in recent years, and there are now radishes that will crop through winter, provided they have a little protection.

Kohl rabi

This is a strange-looking vegetable, but kohl rabi (*Brassica oleracea* Gongylodes Group) is actually a member of the cabbage family. You eat the swollen, tennis-ball-sized stem rather than the leaves. It is a quick-growing plant and is useful as a catch crop or for intercropping between slower maturing crops. But bear in mind that it belongs to the cabbage family and is subject to the same range of pests and diseases, so you must take this into account when you are working out your rotation plan.

from sowing to harvest
5 to 9 weeks.

where to plant
A sunny, open site is preferred, but the kohl rabi plant will tolerate a little shade.

soil preparation
Apply a low-fertility soil improver to poor soil or a medium-soil improver on a reasonably good soil.

sowing and planting
Outdoors sow every 10 to 14 days to provide a continuous supply from summer to autumn. For an early crop sow indoors in modules from late winter to spring and plant out when the plants are around 5 cm (2 in) high.

spacing
Grow in traditional rows 15 cm (6 in) apart in rows that are 30 cm (12 in) apart and in the bed system space at 15 cm (6 in) each way.

care
Hoe regularly between the plants to keep down weeds and water during dry spells, when a mulch of organic matter will help to conserve moisture.

problems
Flea beetle, cabbage root fly and clubroot can all be troublesome.

harvesting and storage
Check the crop regularly and harvest when the stem is somewhere between the size of a golf ball and a tennis ball. Later crops can be left in the ground and lifted in autumn and stored in boxes of sand, like carrots. Kohl rabi can be eaten raw or lightly cooked.

from sowing to harvest

8 to 10 weeks.

where to plant

Grow in a humus-rich, moisture-retentive soil. They will tolerate a little shade in the summer. Oriental brassicas can also be grown as a catch crop between other rows of longer growing brassicas.

soil preparation

If necessary, apply a low-fertility soil improver before sowing or planting.

sowing and planting

Outside sow thinly in shallow drills from early to late summer. For earlier crops sow indoors on a windowsill, then transplant outside when ready.

spacing

Space seeds 15–30 cm (6–12 in) apart each way in both traditonal rows and in the bed system.

care

Water the plants regularly in dry weather and mulch with a low-fertility soil improver to help conserve moisture. If flea beetle is a problem on your allotment, grow Oriental brassicas under horticultural fleece or environmesh.

problems

Flea beetle, slugs, clubroot and caterpillars can all be troublesome.

harvesting and storage

Oriental brassicas can be harvested at any time from seedlings to mature plants. As seedlings they can be used as a cut-and-come-again crop. Some mature plants will regrow after cutting if you leave a stump in the ground. Although they will keep for a few days in the refrigerator, it is better to use them straight away.

There are many oriental brassicas (types of *Brassica rapa*) available now, and they are becoming increasingly popular – they are cultivated mainly for their leaves. Oriental brassicas have similar features to the more commonly grown brassicas, but are generally faster growing. In the right conditions, they are highly productive and take up relatively little space. The choice of plants is varied and includes Chinese cabbage, pak choi, tight-headed Chinese cabbage, oriental mustards, Chinese broccoli and mizuna greens. They all require similar growing conditions.

Oriental brassicas

Turnips

Turnips (*Brassica rapa* Rapifera Group) are one of the easiest of the root crops to grow, and you can harvest them from spring through to late autumn. You can also dig them up and store them for winter use. The flesh is either pink-white or white, and you can eat the young leaves, so nothing goes to waste. They are subject to the same pests and diseases as other brassicas, so turnips need to be incorporated into your crop rotation plan. This is another quick-growing crop that is useful for encouraging children to garden and grow their own food.

from sowing to harvest

Early cultivars around 5 weeks; maincrop cultivars 6 to 10 weeks.

where to plant

Turnips prefer a moist, cool soil and can tolerate some shade. They are a useful plant for catch cropping.

soil preparation

If the soil has been improved for a previous crop, apply a low-fertility soil improver, otherwise use a medium-fertility soil improver or a low-fertility soil improver along with a general organic fertilizer.

sowing and planting

Turnips don't transplant, but an early crop can be had by multi-sowing in modules (5 or 6 seeds per cell in modular trays) in late winter or early spring. Otherwise, start sowing ouside from early spring to autumn at 3 week intervals. Sow in drills 2.5 cm (1 in) deep and cover with horticultural fleece or fine mesh to prevent flea beetles and birds getting to the seedlings. Thin out when the seedlings are around 2.5 cm (1 in) high.

spacing

Plant in rows at 15 cm (6 in) intervals in rows that are 23 cm (9 in) apart. In a bed system spacing should be 15 cm (6 in) each way. Sow seeds in drills at the same spacing and thin plants to similar spacings.

care

Keep the soil between the crops weed-free and water regularly during hot, dry spells or plants may bolt.

problems

Cabbage root fly, flea beetle, clubroot and downy mildew are the main problems that affect turnips.

harvesting and storage

Harvest early turnips when they measure about 5 cm (2 in) across and maincrop types when they about the size of a tennis ball. Turnips will keep in the ground through most winters and can also be stored like carrots (see page 82).

from sowing to harvest
About 26 weeks.

where to plant
An open site in fertile soil that does not dry out readily.

soil preparation
If the soil has been improved for a previous crop, apply a low-fertility soil improver before sowing seeds. If not, apply a general organic fertilizer. Firm the soil where the seedbed is to go before sowing if the soil is loose.

sowing and planting
In milder areas early sowings can be made under horticultural fleece or cloches in late winter for an early crop. Seeds can also be sown in modular trays for transplanting without disturbing the roots. Start sowing outside in drills, 2 cm (¾ in) deep, from mid-spring to early summer. Cover plants with fine mesh or fleece to protect them from flea beetle and pigeons, and thin out when seedling are around 2.5 cm (1 in) high.

spacing
In traditional rows space at 23 cm (9 in) apart in rows that are 38 cm (15 in) apart. In the bed system space 15 x 15 cm (6 x 6 in) each way.

care
Water regularly during dry spells as the roots can turn woody in dry conditions. Conversely, roots can split if they get too much water after a dry spell.

problems
Cabbage root fly, flea beetle, clubroot, white fly and mildew are the main problems that can affect swedes.

harvesting and storage
Begin harvesting when the roots are large enough to use, usually from mid to late autumn onward. Swedes can be left in the ground over winter, but they are likely to become woody. Lift roots and store them in boxes of sand, like carrots (see page 82) and keep in a cool, frost-free place.

Swedes (*Brassica napus* Napobrassica Group) are yet another relative of the cabbage, and newer varieties are a great improvement on older ones, which were just grown as animal feed. It is a hardy crop and will stand through most winters. They are quite sweet to taste and are often used in hearty winter meals and thick soups. Swedes tend to be infested with whitefly, but that is a small price to pay for what is an invaluable winter vegetable. Because swedes are a member of the brassica family they are prone to the same problems as the rest of the family.

Seakale

Seakale (*Crambe maritima*), which was a great favourite of the Victorians, is grown for its blanched shoots that are harvested from mid- to late winter. It has large grey leaves and sweet-scented flowers, which make it an attractive plant. It is not at all difficult to grow, and you can leave it outside to harvest in spring or lift a few roots and force it for winter eating. It is a permanent crop, so even though it is a member of the *Brassicaceae* family, you should put it with other permanent crops in the allotment. As a permanent crop it should last for up to seven years.

from sowing to harvest
Up to 2 years.

where to plant
An open, sunny permanent site in reasonably fertile, well-drained soil with other permanent crops.

soil preparation
Clear all weeds, particularly perennial weeds and, if necessary, apply a medium-fertility soil improver. Test the soil and if it is acid apply lime to raise the pH.

sowing and planting
It's best to grow from seed. As seeds can be slow to germinate, roughen them with sandpaper to aid germination. Sow in early spring in pots and when the seedlings have 3 or 4 leaves select the best plants and plant out. Seeds can be sown outside in a seedbed from early to mid-spring

spacing
Sow in drills 2.5 cm (1 in) deep in rows 30–38 cm (12–15 in) apart. Thin so the plants are 15–23 cm (6–9 in) apart.

care
An annual application each spring of a medium-fertility soil improver or seaweed extract will benefit plants. Remove any yellowing foliage and flowers to divert the plants' energy into producing good roots for forcing.

problems
Slugs, which go for young shoots, and clubroot are the main problems affecting seakale.

harvesting and storage
To grow seakale for blanching leave the plants to grow for at least 1 year before harvesting. To blanch outside in late winter cover the plants with leaves or straw and a bucket to give some protection from the cold. Harvest when the pale stems are 10–20 cm (4–8 in) long. Stop cutting in May. After blanching discard plants and start again. Seakale doesn't keep well, so it is best to eat it fresh from your allotment.

from sowing to harvest

2 to 3 years.

where to plant

Asparagus will grow in a wide range of well-drained soils. Add lime to raise the soil pH if it is below 6.

Soil preparation

Dig over the soil and remove any perennial weeds, and add a medium-fertility soil improver the winter before planting. Add course grit to a heavy clay soil at a rate of 1 barrow load of grit to 3 m² (1.2 yd²) of soil.

sowing and planting

Plants can be raised from seed, but it can take up to 3 years before the plants begin cropping. Sow seeds in modules or pots in late winter in gentle heat, then harden off and plant out in early summer. Alternatively, buy crowns and plant these in spring. Plant out seed-raised plants at a depth of 10 cm (4 in). To plant crowns take out a trench 25 cm (10 in) deep and 30 cm (12 in) wide, making a ridge of soil along the bottom of the trench. When the crowns are in place they should be 10 cm (4 in) below the soil's surface.

spacing

If planting in traditional rows, space plants or crowns 30–40 cm (12–16 in) apart in rows 2 m (6 ft) apart. In the bed system space plants 30 cm (12 in) each way.

care

Keep the plants well-watered in the first year until they become established. Keep the beds weed-free and mulch with a medium-fertility soil improver.

problems

Slugs and root rot are the main problems.

harvesting and storage

Only cut a few spears until the plants become established in the second or third year. The spears are ready to harvest when around 15 cm (6 in) tall; cut them about 2.5 cm (1 in) below soil level. Stop cutting in midsummer to allow the shoots to grow.

Asparagus (*Asparagus officinalis*) is a perennial crop that is becoming increasingly popular. It is expensive to buy, so it's worth making space for this crop on your allotment. Newer cultivars are becoming available that come into cropping earlier than the older cultivars – some will start cropping 2 years after planting rather than 3 or 4 years. If you have heavy clay soil grow asparagus in a raised bed with coarse grit added to improve drainage. The yield of spears can be relatively small, but the plants will crop for 20 years or more.

Many not-so-well-known salad crops, such as land cress, salad rocket, mustard, garden cress, watercress and corn salad, are worth growing to add different flavours to salads and other meals. Each of these leaves has a distinctive flavour. Because they are small and grow quickly you can grow them between rows of slower maturing crops. You can also grow them under cloches through winter. Most of these plants are best used as cut-and-come-again plants, and all except corn salad, which is included here for convenience, belong to the cabbage family, so are best grown with other brassicas.

from sowing to harvest
4 to 12 weeks.

where to plant
A slightly shady place is ideal – the shade from taller brassicas will be sufficient.

soil preparation
Similar soil conditions to other brassicas including a moisture-retentive soil with a medium-fertility soil improver applied for a previous crop.

sowing and planting
Repeated sowings are necessary as these plants can run to seed quickly. Sow seeds in shallow drills every 10 days or so to provide a continuous supply. Early and late sowings can be made under cloches. If the seeds are sown thinly enough there should be no need to thin them further, particularly if grown as a cut-and-come-again crop.

spacing
If sown in drills space the drills 10–15 cm (4–6 in) apart. Alternatively, sow broadcast in wide drills that are about 10–15 cm (4–6 in) wide.

care
Keep the crops well-watered if the soil is dry and pull out any plants that start to produce flowers.

problems
Since all the minor salad crops are quick-growing and are treated most often as cut-and-come-again plants there are few, if any, problems, although, flea beetles and slugs can be troublesome.

harvesting and storage
Begin harvesting as required when the plants are about 8 cm (3 in) tall by cutting, leaving a portion of the stems in the soil to re-grow. These crops don't store at all and should be used fresh from the plants.

from sowing to harvest

Seeds from 2 to 3 years; crowns from 1 to 2 years.

where to plant

Rhubarb requires a deep, fertile soil in sun or part shade and tolerates all but water-logged soils.

soil preparation

Dig soil deeply and apply a medium to high-fertility soil improver before planting. In subsequent years' mulch with a low-fertility soil improver.

sowing and planting

Rhubarb is more easily grown from crowns that can be bought from garden centres, but it can also be raised from seed. Sow seeds under cover in late winter, then harden off and plant out when the threat of frost has passed. Outside sow in spring in drills 2.5 cm (1 in) deep and 30 cm (12 in) apart, then transplant the seedlings to their permanent growing positions in autumn. Plant crowns from autumn to winter.

spacing

Whether planting in traditional rows or the bed system plant crowns at least 1 m (3 ft) apart each way.

care

Water regulary until the plants are well established and remove any flower spikes that appear. Clear away old foliage in winter and mulch with a medium- to high-fertility soil improver.

problems

Rhubarb is usually trouble-free but may suffer from viruses – remove infected plants.

harvesting and storage

Harvest from 12–18 months after planting, but during the second year only take a few stems. Stop harvesting in midsummer. To force rhubarb, harvesting after about 6 weeks, place a bucket over the crowns in winter and pile fresh manure around the bucket – it heats up as it rots down, which speeds up the forcing process. Do not force crowns a second time for at least 2 years to allow the crowns to recover from the forcing process.

Most allotments have a patch of rhubarb (*Rheum cultorum*) stuck in a corner somewhere, but giving this plant a little loving care is well worth the effort. It is easy to grow and you don't need much of it to feed a whole family. It is also quite ornamental, with its large, dramatic leaves and in summer it will produce tall flower spikes, which you should cut off. It is the pinkish-red stems that you eat. Rhubarb is a long-lived plant, so it is well worth doing thorough soil preparation before planting.

Fruit

Introduction

Growing fruit is one of the most rewarding aspects of gardening. Sitting under the shade of an apple tree in summer after a hard day's work is one of life's great pleasures. Fresh fruit from the garden is better than any fast food you can buy and will reinvigorate you on a tiring day. Moreover, apples, pears and plums give an astonishing display of spring blossom, offering the mouthwatering prospects of fruits later in the season. In some years there may not be so much fruit, but that is more than made up for in other years, when there is a bountiful harvest. Yes, growing fruit is still worth all the effort.

There is, of course, the problem of choosing cultivars, and there is not the space in this book to give long lists of recommended cultivars. For best results talk to local growers, see what is cropping well on other allotments in the area and, above all, ask about them. Most allotment-holders are only too pleased to stop and have a cup of tea and a chat. Visit gardens and contact organizations such as Garden Organic, whose experts will tell you the best varieties to choose for your area, because a cultivar that does well in one area may not do so well in another. Specialist fruit nurseries are a mine of information, too, and some organizations have fruit-tasting days, when you can go along and taste different varieties to see which ones you like best.

Remember that most fruit trees are grafted on to rootstocks to regulate their growth, so rootstocks for each fruit are recommended with each entry here. However, the rootstocks used may vary depending on the country you live in and the weather conditions in your area.

Bare-rooted plants should be planted during their dormant period, from late autumn to early spring. Container-grown plants, even those bearing fruit, can be planted at any time of the year if the soil conditions permit, but bear in mind that container-grown trees require extra attention, especially in terms of watering, than bare-rooted trees. Bare-rooted trees tend to be slightly cheaper than container-grown trees and generally have larger root systems. Whether your new plant is container grown or a bare-rooted example, it is worth treating it well right from the start because it will be there for a long time.

Stake new trees at planting time (see page 66) and check tree ties on stakes regularly to make sure they are not too tight.

Fruit trees need regular pruning to keep them healthy and cropping well, and plants trained as cordons, espaliers or fans will require pruning and tying in to their supports (see pages 66–7). In general, remember that the harder you prune, the stronger the resulting growth will be.

Left Mouth-watering fruits, such as blackberries, are a highlight of the summer allotment.

Apples (*Malus domestica*) are one of the most popular fruits to grow – the trees are beautiful in flower, and you get the bonus of delicious fruits in the autumn. Most apples grow well on a rich, free-draining soil, but if your soil is poor you can use a tree on a more vigorous rootstock to compensate for the poorer soil conditions. Different types of rootstocks (the roots the cultivar is grafted on to) determine the vigour or ultimate size of the tree. Apples can be trained in many ways, including cordons, fans and espaliers.

soil preparation and planting

On light soils dig a hole 1m (3 ft) in diameter, and on heavy soils a hole twice that diameter. Knock in a 1 m (3 ft) long stake, off-centre. Loosen the subsoil with a fork – on heavy soils also loosen the soil round the sides of the hole. Fill a bucket with well-rotted manure or compost and mix it into the soil you removed to make the hole. Place the tree next to the stake, so it sits no deeper than when it was previously planted (a darker mark at the base of the tree shows previous planting depth). Backfill with the soil and manure mix firming as you go, then secure the tree to its stake. Plant bare-rooted trees from late autumn to late winter and container grown trees anytime of the year.

spacing

Space standard trees and bush and espalier trained trees 2.5–3 m (8–10 ft) apart, depending on the rootstock used. Cordons should be planted 75 cm (30 in) apart.

rootstocks

M27 is very dwarfing, M9 is dwarfing, and both these need staking for most of their lives. M26 is more vigorous and good on poorer soils.

care

Keep weeds at bay and conserve moisture by using mulches like straw 8–10 cm (3–4 in) deep. Once established, trees will benefit from winter pruning – trained forms like cordons and espaliers will need extra pruning in summer to encourage fruiting buds. Start thinning about 6 weeks after the petals have fallen.

problems

In late spring hang up pheromone traps for codling moth, check foliage for mildew, and look out for aphids on young shoots.

harvesting and storage

Fruits begin ripening from late summer to late autumn. Test for ripeness by cupping the fruits in your hand and gently twisting. If ripe they will come away easily. You can eat early cultivars right away. Late cultivars need to be stored in a cool, dark and frost-free place.

soil preparation and planting

On light soils dig a hole 1m (3 ft) in diameter, and on heavy soils a hole twice that diameter. Knock in a 1 m (3 ft) long stake, off-centre. Loosen the subsoil with a fork – on heavy soils also loosen the soil round the sides of the hole. Fill a bucket with well-rotted manure or compost and mix it into the soil you removed to make the hole. Place the tree next to the stake, so it sits no deeper than when it was previously planted (a darker mark at the base of the tree shows previous planting depth). Backfill with the soil and manure mix firming as you go, then secure the tree to its stake. Plant bare-rooted trees from late autumn to late winter and container grown trees anytime of the year.

spacing

Pear trees require similar spacing to apple trees (see opposite).

rootstocks

Quince C is a dwarfing rootstock and suitable for all forms of tree. Quince A is semi-dwarfing and is suitable for growing trees on poorer soils.

care

Keep weeds at bay and conserve moisture by using mulches like straw 8–10 cm (3–4 in) deep. Once established, trees will benefit from winter pruning trained forms like cordons and espaliers will need extra pruning in summer to encourage fruiting buds. It may be necessary to thin fruits as for apples (see opposite).

problems

Look out for aphids on young shoots and use a jet of water to wash them off. Pears are also affected by leaf blister mite, which attacks young foliage, and pear larvae that may be present in young fruits.

harvesting and storage

Judging the ripeness of pears can be difficult. As for apples, cup the fruit in your hands and gently twist. If it comes away easily the fruit is ready for picking, but not necessarily ripe – some cultivars need to ripen off the tree. Store pears in a cool, dark and frost-free place where they will keep until the following spring, a least.

Pears (*Pyrus communis*) require similar conditions to apples, but enjoy warmer growing conditions. The earliest cultivars are ready to eat in midsummer and can be eaten straight from the tree. Most are picked from early to mid-autumn and need about 3 weeks after picking to ripen. Late-storing pears will keep well into winter in cool, dark and frost-free conditions. As the flowers are produced earlier than apples, the flowers are more susceptible to frost damage than apples and may need protecting. Keep some horticultural fleece handy.

A plum tree (*Prunus domestica*) laden with fruit is a sight to behold. The fruits ripen from late summer to autumn, but the flowers appear earlier than both apples and pears, from early to mid-spring, making them susceptible to frost damage, so it is unlikely that you will get a great crop every year, but this makes them all the more enjoyable. Plums are usually grown as free-standing trees, but they can be grown as fans and cordons (see page 63). They are not too fussy about soil as long as the drainage is good.

soil preparation and planting

Plums prefer an open site but sheltered from cold winds. Good drainage is essential. On light soils dig a hole 1 m (3 ft) in diameter, and on heavy soils a hole twice that diameter. Knock in a 1 m (3 ft) long stake, off-centre. Loosen the subsoil with a fork – on heavy soils also loosen the soil round the sides of the hole. Fill a bucket with well-rotted manure or compost and mix it into the soil you removed to make the hole. Place the tree next to the stake, so it sits no deeper than when it was previously planted (a darker mark at the base of the tree shows previous planting depth). Backfill with the soil mix, firming as you go, then secure the tree to its stake. Plant plums as the same time as apples and pears (see pages 122 and 123).

spacing

Follow the same advice as for apples (see page 122) and pears (see page 123).

rootstocks

Pixie is a dwarfing rootstock that crops after 3 years. The trees will eventually grow to about 2.4 m (8 ft) high. St Julien A is a semi-dwarfing rootstock that makes a larger tree than Pixie. It will also start cropping in 3 years.

care

Once established, trees will benefit from pruning. Plums are susceptible to silver leaf disease, so do all pruning between spring and early autumn and not winter. Prune out all dead or diseased wood and branches that are crossing or rubbing. In a good year there may be a mass of fruit and some thinning will be necessary. After the fruits naturally drop thin the remaining fruits to around 5–10 cm (2–4 in) apart.

problems

Plums are affected by silver leaf disease, caterpillars, frost damage, birds, wasps and some species of aphids.

harvesting and storage

Look for fruits that are fully coloured. A ripe fruit will pull away easily from the tree. Plums don't store well but can be used in preserves.

soil preparation and planting

Grapes prefer a slightly alkaline (limy) soil, with organic matter applied to help retain moisture. Soil that has a high-nutrient content is not desirable, as it will make plants produce a lot of growth at the expense of fruits, and on poor soils you will need to improve the drainage before planting. This can be done by adding well-rotted manure or compost at 125 g per sq m (4 oz per 3 sq ft) – a small handful of bonemeal is also beneficial. Mix the manure or compost and bonemeal with the soil you removed to make the planting hole. Plant to the original soil mark on the stem. Plant grapes at anytime of the year. Grapes can be trained against walls or on wires and there are various support systems you can use. Described below is the Double Guyot system.

spacing

Plant grapes around 1.4 m (4 ft) apart.

care

Training is relatively straightforward using the Double Guyot system using wires. In the first year cut back young stems to about 15 cm (6 in); in summer tie in the leading shoot vertically and pinch back sideshoots to 5 or 6 leaves; in winter cut back all growth to a bud approximately 40 cm (16 in) from soil level. In the second year allow 3 buds to grow and tie the growths to a vertical stake. Pinch back any sideshoots as before. In the winter tie the shoots to the bottom wires and shorten the growths to leave shoots about 60 cm (24 in) long. Prune the central shoot to leave 3 buds. The following season shoots will grow from the horizontal growths – tie these in vertically. Pinch back the shoots when they reach the top wire and remove any sideshoots. Tie in 3 new shoots that grow from the central shoot to the vertical stake. These are tied down on to the horizontal wires the following winter.

problems

The two main problems are downy mildew and grey mould (*botrytis*).

harvesting and storage

Harvest when the grapes are fully coloured by cutting through the stalk about 2.5 cm (1 in) from the bunch. Eat grapes soon after harvesting.

Grapes (*Vitis vinifera*) can be expensive to buy, but they are quite easy to grow. They are hardy plants but need warmth to ripen the fruits. Vines grow vigorously, so keep them in check through regular pruning and trimming. There are separate cultivars for making wine and for using as dessert grapes. In cooler areas it may be best to stick to dessert grapes, as they take less time to ripen. Although they require a bit of effort with pruning and trimming, grapes are very rewarding to grow and the taste of grapes picked fresh from the vine is incomparable with anything bought from a shop.

Strawberries

Strawberries (*Fragaria spp.*) are probably most people's favourite summer fruit – the first strawberry of the year is simply sublime. They are not a permanent crop, and you might want to include them in a rotation plan, since strawberries need to be renewed every 3 years and moved to different soil. However, often it is more effective to renew a few plants every year. If you choose cultivars carefully you can have strawberries from early summer through to autumn, but if space is limited plant just 2–3 cultivars.

soil preparation and planting

Choose an open site for planting in early autumn or spring. Strawberries are not fussy about soil type, but highly fertile soils encourage foliage at the expense of fruits. If the soil is poor, apply a low-fertility soil improver before planting. To plant, take out a hole large enough to take the roots if a bare-rooted plant, or for the root ball if it is pot-grown. Plant so the crown (where the roots and foliage are joined) is at or just above soil level. Water in well.

spacing

In traditional rows space plants 30–45 cm (12–18 in) apart in the row with 75 cm (30 in) between rows. If using a bed system space plants at 30 cm (12 in) apart each way. Space around the plants encourages good air circulation, which reduces the possibility of disease.

care

Water occassionally during normal conditions but keep plants well watered during dry spells, particularly while the fruits are swelling. Place straw beneath the fruits to protect them from soil splashes. After you have picked the fruits cut off the foliage and remove the straw to encourage new growths. In early autumn remove most of the runners (long wiry stems with plantlets on the ends), keeping 2 or 3 for propagating more plants.

problems

Buy stock that is certified as being free from virus, and if you propagate your own plants from runners, make sure the parent plants are healthy. A virus usually manifests as stunted growth and mosaic-patterns on the foliage, so if you do have a virus remove and destroy any infected plants. Grey mould (*botrytis*) is one of the main problems that can affect strawberries – pick off any infected berries and lay down straw. Powdery mildew can be a problem in dry weather, so keep the plants well watered. Check the plants regularly for aphids and rub off any you see. Net the fruits as they begin to swell to protect them from birds

harvesting and storage

Harvest strawberries when they are fully coloured. Fruits can be made into preserves.

soil preparation and planting

Raspberries prefer a free-draining, slightly acidic soil. On poor soils add compost or manure at up to 2 large barrow loads per 5 sq m (50 sq ft). Remove all perennial weeds and erect a post and wire support. Use posts that will stand 1.5 m (5 ft) above ground and attach 3 horizontal wires stretched evenly between the posts. Set the stools (young individual canes) so the roots are just below soil level – raspberries are shallow rooting and don't like being planted deeply. Plant from late autumn to late winter.

spacing

Plant the stools 38–45 cm (15–18 in) apart in the rows and space the rows at least 1.2–1.5 m (4–5 ft) apart.

care

Keep down weeds and watch out for signs of pests and diseases. An annual application of compost or manure should be all that is necessary for feeding. During the first year tie the canes to the support wires as they grow and remove all flowers that form so there is no cropping. In subsequent years cut out old canes once fruited and tie in the new ones (see page 64). Cut off any shoots that grow outside the row. Use straw or hay as a mulch between the rows.

problems

Start by buying healthy, virus-free stock. If virus is present on your allotment don't grow raspberries in the same spot for at least 6 years. Virus' shows as mottling or a mosaic pattern on the leaves – destroy any affected plants. Grey mould (*botrytis*) can also be troublesome. Look for aphids throughout the season and squash them with your hands. Net the plants to prevent birds getting at the fruits.

harvesting and storage

Harvest when the fruits are fully coloured and pull away from the plant easily, leaving the centre of the fruit on the plant. Raspberries will keep in the fridge for a few days, but are best eaten fresh.

Raspberries (*Rubus idaeus*) usually start to ripen a little later than strawberries, so extending the season of delicious summer fruits. They are usually grown in rows and take up a lot of room, but if space is limited you can still fit some in by putting in a 1.5 m (5 ft) stake and grouping a few plants around this. As well as the usual summer-fruiting varieties, there are autumn-fruiting ones that can be grown without wires. Summer raspberries produce fruit on canes grown the previous year, but autumn cultivars produce fruits on canes produced in the current year.

People often go blackberry-hunting in autumn as blackberries (*Rubus fruticosus*) grow wild, but it is easy to grow your own. During the last century many crosses between blackberries and raspberries were made, resulting in a group called hybrid berries, which includes loganberries, tayberries, tummelberries and boysenberries. These tend to crop earlier than blackberries, but have a similar growth habit and growing requirements. They will begin cropping in the second year after planting and every year after that.

soil preparation and planting

Blackberries and hybrid berries require similar growing conditions and support systems to raspberries (see page 127). While blackberries can be grown in partial shade, all hybrid berries prefer full sun. If the soil is poor incorporate manure or compost at up to two large barrow loads per 5 sq m (50 sq ft) before planting. If growing at the side of a fence or shed prepare a bed at least 1 m (3 ft) wide. Plant bare-rooted cultivars from late autumn to late winter and container-grown cultivars at any time of the year.

spacing

Erect posts as for raspberries, but use more wires setting them 23 cm (9 in) apart (see page 127). A similar arrangement will be needed against a fence or shed. Allow up to 7.2 m (24 ft) between plants as they are vigorous growers. Plant each stool (young individual cane) with the roots just below soil level.

care

In the first year only a few canes will grow. Tie these to one side like half a fan – by summer this will be a weekly task. These canes will fruit the following year. In the second year tie in new canes to the other side of the fruiting canes to complete the fan – these canes will fruit the following year. Cut out fruiting canes once the fruits have been harvested, and repeat the process every year. If growth is poor mulch in winter or spring with compost or manure, as described above.

problems

Plant only healthy, virus-free stock. Grey mould (*botrytis*) may be troublesome, but generally these berries are trouble-free. Any plants showing signs of virus – mottling of foliage – should be destroyed. Cover the crop with netting to prevent birds getting the fruits.

harvesting and storage

Harvest blackberries when they are fully coloured. When they are picked the core should remain intact. Berries are best eaten fresh from the plant, and all berries can be made into preserves.

soil preparation and planting

Red and whitecurrants aren't fussy about soil, but if it is poor soil apply a low-fertility soil improver at 10 litre (2 gallons) per sq m (10 sq ft) before planting. If you're growing them as cordons put up wires as support. A post and wire system similar to that for raspberries is also fine (see page 127) – it's an ideal way of growing them if space is limited. Look for well-balanced plants that have good root systems and no sign of pests or diseases, and plant so the root ball is just below soil level. Plants can be bought as bushes or partly trained as cordons or fans, but it's fun buying one-year-old bushes and training them to shape yourself. Plant bare-rooted bushes from late autumn to late winter and container-grown plants at any time of the year.

spacing

Plant bushes 1.2–1.5 m (4–5 ft) apart; fans 2 m (6 ft) apart; and cordons 40–45 cm (16–18 in) apart.

care

Keep well watered until plants become established and in dry conditions. Summer prune sideshoots (spurs) to 5 leaves in late summer. In winter these spurs can be further shortened to 2 or 3 buds – this promotes production of fruiting spurs. Leave the leading shoots until winter and prune by half to a third depending on how vigourously the plant grows. These shoots form the basic framework of the bushes. In spring mulch plants with hay or straw to suppress weeds and retain moisture in the soil. The application of compost every 3 years should be adequate feeding.

problems

Watch out for leaf blister aphid that cause distinctive blistering of the foliage and pick off any infested leaves. Gooseberry sawfly larvae can quickly defoliate a plant and powdery mildew can affect young growths. Pick off sawfly larvae and cut off any mildewed leaves. Cover with netting to prevent birds eating the fruits.

harvesting and storage

Harvest when each 'string' of fruits is fully coloured, picking off the whole bunch. Eat berries fresh or make them into preserves or jellies.

A redcurrant (*Ribes rubrum*) bush full of ripe fruits is a stunning sight. They are versatile fruits, and you can use them fresh from the plants or use them to make jelly or jam. You can use whitecurrants (*Ribes rubrum*) in the same way, and they require exactly the same treatment as redcurrants. Both these currants produce fruit on short shoots that grow from a permanent framework of branches, or fruiting spurs, like those on apple trees. This makes them easy to train as cordons (single-stemmed) or as fans (see page 63), so they don't take up a lot of space and the bushes will last for many years.

Blackcurrants (*Ribes nigrum*) are nutritious and reliable fruits, which can be eaten raw, cooked or used in preserves. They have a high vitamin C content, and as with other soft fruits, it is best to eat them as soon as possible after picking. Blackcurrants are grown as bushes and cannot be trained into other forms, such as fans or cordons. Although they take up a fair amount of space, they are well worth growing. Jostaberries, a hybrid between blackcurrants and gooseberries, are cultivated in the same way as blackcurrants.

soil preparation and planting

Blackcurrants need quite fertile conditions, but otherwise are not fussy about soil type. They can be planted at any time of the year and are generally sold as 1- or 2-year-old plants grown in containers. Bare-root plants can only be planted during the dormant season (late autumn to late winter).Clear the site of perennial weeds, and if the soil is poor, dig in well-rotted manure at the rate of 1 bucketful to 2 sq m (20 sq ft), or compost at twice that rate. Plant so that 7–10 cm (3–4 in) of the stems are below soil level. New shoots will grow from below soil level each year.

spacing

Set the plants at 1.5–1.8 m (5–6 ft) apart.

care

Immediately after planting cut 1-year-old bushes to just above soil level to encourage strong, new growths, then keep the plants well watered until they become established. Blackcurrants fruit mainly on wood that at is least two years old, so the aim of pruning is to encourage new wood while still retaining a framework of existing shoots. Aim to remove about a third of all shoots every year. It is inevitable that you will remove some fruiting wood, but you have to maintain a balance between new and old wood. Pruning can be done just after harvesting, but is best done in winter when the leaves have fallen, as it's easier to see what you are doing. Mulch in late-spring with straw or hay, and feed with compost, well-rotted manure or organic fertilizer every 3 years.

problems

Plant healthy, virus-free plants and cultivars that are resistant to big bug mite and mildew. Grey mould (*botrytis*) may be a problem on ripening fruits.

harvesting and storage

Begin to harvest with the 'strings' of fruit are fully coloured. Eat the fruits fresh or use in preserves.

soil preparation and planting

As gooseberries and redcurrants are closely related they require similar soil conditions (see page 129). Site the bushes where there is a good airflow to prevent diseases and keep well watered until the plants become established. Bare-rooted bushes are planted from autumn to spring and container-grown plants at any time of the year. Plant so the root ball of container-grown plants is just below soil level. With bare-rooted bushes, plant to the previous level, which will show as a soil mark low down on the main stem.

spacing

Space bushes in a similar way to redcurrants (see page 129). For cordons set the plants at 30 cm (12 in) apart, and for fans at around 1.5 m (5 ft) apart.

care

Feed and water gooseberries as you would for redcurrants (see page 129). Gooseberries have rather lax or weeping growths, which, if they touch the soil, can lead to fungal infections. To avoid this and to give the new shoots some support always prune to upward facing buds and place 3 or 4 stakes around the bushes to tie new growths to with string. Prune sideshoots back to 5 or 6 buds in late summer or early autumn and prune again to 3 or 4 buds in winter. In winter growths (shoots) at the tips of branches are pruned by half to a third – these shoots form the main framework of branches. In winter also prune out any branches congesting the centre of the bushes

Another way to reduce the problem of lax or weeping growth is to train the plants as cordons or fans, pruning as described above. If growing in either of these ways you will need to post and wire supports similar to redcurrants.

problems

Gooseberries are affected by gooseberry sawfly, American gooseberry mildew, aphids and birds.

harvesting and storage

Fruits are best eaten soon after harvesting, but can be frozen or made into preserves.

Gooseberries (*Ribes uva-crispa* var. *reclinatum*) are the first fruits to ripen in summer. You can train them as cordons or fans (see page 63), so they don't take up a lot of space. They are quite thorny, so be careful when you are working with the bushes. Gooseberries and redcurrants are closely related and require similar growing conditions and pruning. Gooseberries will tolerate some shade, but to get the best flavour grow them in full sun. The bushes will last for many years, and 1-year-old bushes will start cropping in the second or third year after planting.

Herbs

Introduction

No organic allotment should be without a few herbs, and they will add a new dimension to the enjoyment of your allotment. They are easy to grow, attractive to look at, can be eaten and will attract beneficial insects. In most cases it is the leaves that are used, but different parts such as roots, fruits, seeds and flowers can also be eaten, depending on the type of plant. It is probably best to have a dedicated area for growing herbs, because most of them are perennial. Annual and biennial herbs, such as parsley and chervil, should not be grown in the same spot every year – so create a 'crop rotation' section in the herb garden, or include them in the main vegetable beds. The herbs listed are just a basic selection; there are many more you can try.

If you want to make a formal herb garden on the allotment it's worth taking time over it and working out a plan on paper first (see page 20). It is best to group herbs by their growing requirements rather than by their use. Although most herbs require a sunny spot, others will tolerate some shade.

Maintaining herbs

Thorough preparation is essential before planting your herbs. Make sure you dig out any perennial weeds like dandelions (*Taraxicum officinale*). If your soil is heavy clay incorporate coarse grit at a rate of 2 large barrow loads per 5 m² (6 yd²) to improve drainage. You will need to do some watering to get the plants established, but after that little watering should be necessary because most herbs come from the drier regions of the world. Keep weeds down by hand-weeding between the plants. Some woody or shrub-like herbs, such as thyme and rosemary, will require some pruning after flowering to keep them compact. The flavour of herbs is better if they are not allowed to produce flowers. You can propagate all herbs from seeds, cuttings and by division.

Below A healthy well-stocked herb garden looks good, attracts wildlife and supplies tasty kitchen flavourings.

Chives (*Allium schoenoprasum*) are deservedly popular. They are easy to grow from seeds and division, and their attractive flowerheads make them a superb edging plant for the herb area. Chives prefer moist soil and a position in good light. You can sow seeds outside in early spring or divide established plants every 3–4 years in spring or autumn. Harvest the chives by cutting them with scissors. They thrive on this and the more you cut them the more you get.

Dill (*Anethum graveolens*) is an attractive hardy annual culinary herb, which will seed itself naturally in milder areas, but in colder areas it is better to sow seeds every year. It has feathery leaves and yellow flowers, making it as suitable for ornamental borders of the allotment. Dill prefers a well-drained soil in a sunny position. Sow seeds in drills 30 cm (12 in) apart in mid-spring and thin the plants to 30 cm (12 in) apart. Sow in succession at monthly intervals until midsummer for a continuous crop. Hoe between the plants in summer and water if required. Pick the leaves as you need them in spring and summer and cut seedheads as they ripen.

Chervil Another annual herb that will self-seed freely, chervil (*Anthriscus cerefolium*) is not the most attractive-looking of herbs, resembling as it does rather unruly parsley. Nevertheless, its spicy, aniseed flavour makes it one of the most useful in the kitchen. Chervil grows best in a slightly shady, cooler area as it has a tendency to run to seed quickly in warm conditions. Sow seeds from early to mid-spring in drills 20 cm (8 in) apart and thin out the seedlings to the same spacing. You can also sow seeds in autumn, but these plants will need to be covered with cloches in winter.

Chives

Dill

Chervil

Horseradish A vigorous, hardy perennial, horseradish (*Armoracia rusticana*) has leaves that resemble those of docks. It is the white roots that are edible, but be warned, they are very hot. Horseradish likes a rich soil and a position in sun or semi-shade. Whatever you do, keep it in check – it will take over the whole allotment if you let it. Grow it in a raised bed or in a large pot to restrict the roots. Buy some roots or take root cuttings about 15 cm (6 in) long and plant them vertically in spring. Horseradish needs no encouragement to grow! In autumn lift roots as you need them. You can store them in pots or boxes of damp sand or old potting compost.

Tarragon Both French tarragon (*Artemisia dracunculus*) and Russian tarragon (*A. dracunculus* subsp. *dracunculoides*) are hardy perennial herbs that require a sunny position in well-drained soil. Russian tarragon is the more vigorous and will withstand colder winters. French tarragon has a far better flavour. French tarragon will not grow from seed, and you will need to buy in young plants or take cuttings from existing plants in spring and summer. You can divide older plants in spring. Weed and water through the summer as required, and in winter protect with a layer of straw or other organic matter. Lift and divide every 3–4 years to maintain vigour. Pick fresh leaves as and when required. You can dry the leaves, but they do lose some of their flavour.

Caraway

Fennel

Caraway A biennial herb, needing two seasons to grow well, caraway (*Carum carvi*) requires a sunny position and well-drained soil. The aromatic seeds are often used in baking, confectionery and in meat stews. You can also add the leaves to soups and salads. Gather the leaves when they are young and collect the seedheads in summer. Propagate by sowing seeds in spring, summer or autumn.

Fennel The herb fennel (*Foeniculum vulgare*) should not be confused with Florence fennel (see page 85), which is grown for its swollen stem bases. The herb is a hardy perennial, grown for its leaves and seeds. It is a tall, stately plant with fine, feathery foliage and bright yellow flowers, which look as attractive in flower borders as on the allotment. It is also good for attracting predators to control pests. There is also a bronze-leaved variety, *F. vulgare* 'Purpureum'. The leaves and seeds have an aniseed flavour. Fennel prefers a good, fertile soil and plenty of sun. Sow seeds in autumn or spring and thin out to 60 cm (24 in) apart. Divide clumps in spring or autumn, planting the divisions at the same spacing. Keep the plants trimmed to provide a succession of young leaves, but leave a few shoots to grow on to flower and produce seeds to collect later. Harvest the leaves fresh, as they don't keep after harvesting. Hang some stems up in a cool, airy shed later in autumn to dry the seeds.

Hyssop (*Hyssopus officinalis*) is a shrubby perennial herb that has spikes of purple-blue flowers. It needs well-drained, neutral to alkaline soil, so apply some lime if necessary. You can use the leaves to flavour stews, soups, game and bean dishes. Gather young, fresh leaves any time and hang up a few in a cool shed to dry. Sow seeds in autumn or spring or take softwood cuttings, about 8 cm (3 in) long, from the tips of the shoots in summer.

Bay or sweet bay (*Laurus nobilis*) is one of the most ornamental plants you can get if you keep it trimmed to a nice shape. It can be tender in some colder areas, but plants can last in gardens for many years. If you are uncertain, grow it in a container so that you can move it under cover in late autumn to protect it from winter frosts. Bay leaves resemble those of laurel, but they are, of course, edible, whereas laurel leaves are poisonous. Bay is easily identified by the distinctive smell of the leaves. It prefers semi-shade, and if you grow it in a container use a soil-based compost. You can buy trees of all sizes or take cuttings from existing trees in summer. Keep the trees well watered at all times. You can let them grow naturally or trim them to fancy shapes. If grown in a pot feed once a month with liquid manure. Pick leaves as and when required; you can also dry them and store them in airtight jars.

Basil

Mint

Basil (*Ocimum basilicum*) is a perennial but is more often grown as an annual. Sweet basil tends to have a better flavour than bush basil, but there are many types. All types prefer a sunny site in good, fertile, well-drained soil. Sow seeds in pots indoors in spring, pot on and harden off in a cold frame. Plant out when the threat of frost has passed, spacing plants 30 cm (12 in) apart. In cooler areas you may have to grow plants under cover or cloches. Keep the plants well watered and pinch out the growing tips to keep them compact. Harvest the leaves through summer or you can freeze them in ice cubes.

Mint There are many different types of mint (*Mentha*), which is one of the most popular of herbs. It is perennial, but the foliage dies down each winter. Applemint (*M. suaveolens*) and spearmint (*M. spicata*) are the best for cooking. Mint can be invasive, so it is better to grow it in pots sunk into the ground – leave the rim of the pot about 5 cm (2 in) above soil level. If growing it directly in the ground you will have to keep it in check by cutting back both stems and roots. Mint will grow in practically any soil – it is difficult to kill! Plant young mint plants in the spring and they will grow quickly. Pick regularly to keep the plants in check. At the end of the season dig up a few roots and pot them up. They will grow through the winter on a windowsill or in a greenhouse for winter use. The leaves freeze well in ice cubes.

Coriander (*Coriandrum sativum*) is a hardy annual herb, which has attractive, divided foliage and small white or pale mauve flowers. Different cultivars are available for growing from foliage or from seed. Coriander does best in sun, although it will tolerate semi-shade, and in rich, but well-drained soil. The plants have a rather unpleasant smell, so don't grow them indoors. Pick the young leaves to use fresh or freeze them. Gather the seedheads as they ripen. Propagate by sowing seeds in spring.

Parsley (*Petroselinum crispum*) is one of the most popular and useful herbs. There are many cultivars with either plain or crinkled leaves, and which you choose is down to personal preference, but they're all good. Parsley is more usually grown as an annual, but it will last for several seasons and will often seed itself freely. It prefers a little shade and a lot of moisture, because it runs to seed very quickly if it gets dry at the roots. Sow seeds from early winter indoors and from spring to autumn outdoors in shallow drills, spacing plantlets 15 cm (6 in) apart. Sow again in midsummer for a continuous supply into autumn and grow in pots for winter use indoors. Remove weeds and keep the plants watered through the summer. Parsley is in the carrot family, and is prone to carrot fly. Cut the leaves as and when required, but just take a few from each plant at one time. To store, you can freeze the leaves in ice cubes.

Sage The culinary herb sage (*Salvia officinalis*) is an attractive shrub to grow on the allotment. Sage has pretty blue flowers and the leaves come in various shades, from greenish-purple to almost yellow, and some are variegated. Sage prefers a sunny position and well-drained soil, so to improve drainage, dig in 2 barrow loads of course grit to 5 m² (6 yd²) of soil if you have clay soil. Buy young plants and plant them out in spring 60 cm (24 in) apart. Sage can be propagated easily from cuttings taken in summer, 8 cm (3 in) long. Pinch back shoots in summer to keep the plants compact. Pick fresh leaves as required and pick shoots off and hang them up in a cool shed to dry.

Marjoram Wild marjoram (*Origanum vulgare*) and pot marjoram (*O. onites*) are hardy perennials. Sweet marjoram (*O. majorana*), which has the best flavour, is not as hardy as the species and is usually grown as a half-hardy annual. All are used widely as culinary herbs. All types grow best in sunny positions. They prefer well-drained soil, but dislike being too dry, so incorporate plenty of organic matter before planting. Plant out young plants or divisions from established plants 30 cm (12 in) apart in spring. Sow seeds of sweet marjoram in spring in heat indoors and plant out 20 cm (8 in) apart when the threat of frost has passed. Pinch out growing tips regularly to maintain a bushy habit and water if necessary. Lift and pot up some for winter use and divide perennials every 3 years. Pick leaves fresh as and when you require them. Sweet marjoram dries well and all types freeze well.

Chamomile (*Chamaemelum nobile*) is a hardy, dense, creeping, evergreen perennial. It needs a sunny site and prefers light, well-drained soil. It is good planted at the edge of beds, where you get the wonderful scent as you brush the foliage as you walk by. It can also be used as an ornamental lawn instead of grass outside the shed. Seeds can be sown in spring or autumn. Divide established plants in spring. The apple-scented leaves can be used in pot-pourri and the aromatic flowers can be used in herbal tea. Pick the leaves as and when you require them. Gather flowers when they are fully open in summer and dry them whole.

Borage (*Borago officinalis*) is a hardy annual, which freely seeds itself every year. However, to make sure you have it, sow seeds each spring. It is another decorative herb, with arching shoots and sprays of deep blue or white flowers, making it at home in a flower border as well as on the allotment. It is also terrific for attracting bees. Borage needs an open, sunny position and will not grow well in shade, but it is tolerant of a wide range of soil conditions. Sow seeds in mid-spring and thin the plants to 38 cm (15 in) apart. It will die down in winter and any seeds in the soil will regrow in spring. Remove seedlings growing where you don't want them. Borage needs no encouragement to grow, so trim the plant regularly to keep it in check. Pick young leaves in summer. The cucumber-flavoured leaves can be added to salads and the flowers to cold drinks. The leaves can be frozen – they don't dry well.

Savory

Summer savory (*Satureja hortensis*) is an annual, and winter savory (*S. montana*) is a shrubby, evergreen perennial, and both are good for attracting bees. Savories need a sunny position and well-drained soil. Sow seeds of summer and winter savory outside in spring in drills 15 cm (6 in) apart. You can increase the shrubby type by taking cuttings in summer. Space plants 45 cm (18 in) apart. Summer savory doesn't need much attention, apart from weeding and watering when necessary. Winter savory needs occasional trimming to prevent it from becoming leggy. Pick leaves of summer savory through the season. You can pick shrubby savory throughout the year.

Rosemary

(*Rosmarinus officinalis*) will make quite a large evergreen shrub if you allow it to. It is a delightful herb, with a strong, pleasant smell, and trimmed, makes an ideal small hedge to edge your herb area. It produces velvety, blue flowers, and there are several variegated forms, as well as cultivars with pink and white flowers. It does best in a sunny position in well-drained but moisture-retentive soil. You can plant out container-grown plants at any time, setting them 60 cm (24 in) apart. You can also take cuttings in summer – they root very easily. Trim back the plants after flowering to keep them compact. Rosemary will provide fresh leaves all year round, so there is no point in storing or preserving them. Rosemary is most widely used as a culinary herb.

Lovage (*Levisticum officinale*) is a shrubby perennial. It is a tall plant, to 1.8 m (6 ft), and needs a lot of space to grow. The topgrowth dies down each year. All parts of the plant are strongly flavoured, so it is one to experiment with. It will tolerate partial shade, but does better in full sun. Add well-rotted manure to the soil, because lovage needs a lot of moisture. Sow seeds in spring or divide established clumps in spring or autumn. Lovage needs no encouragement to grow – it's very vigorous. Harvest leaves through the summer and autumn to add to soups, stocks and stews. You can dry the leaves by hanging them up in bunches in a cool, dry shed.

Thyme There are many different type of thyme (*Thymus spp.*), from low-growing, ground-hugging plants to small shrubs. They are all excellent for attracting pollinating insects to the allotment. Thyme prefers a sunny site and well-drained soil. It does best in neutral soil, with a pH of 7. You can raise common thyme (*T. vulgaris*) from seeds, but it's easier to buy in young plants and take cuttings in summer to increase your stock. You can plant out plants bought in pots at any time, spacing them 30 cm (12 in) apart – the plants will spread out to cover the ground. Pinch out the tips regularly, so that plants do not become leggy, and cut back hard after flowering. Pick the leaves fresh through the summer, although the flavour is better when the leaves are dried. Use thyme to flavour soups, sauces, stocks and meat dishes. Cut shoots off before flowering and hang them up in a cool, airy shed to dry.

trouble-shooting

There is no doubt that growing your fruit and vegetables organically and cutting out the use of pesticides is far better for you, but it is not a panacea for all problems and plants will still be attacked by pests and diseases. There are a number of so-called organic chemicals, but some of these can be just as toxic as their synthetic counterparts. However, there are ways of controlling problems without recourse to synthetic chemicals. Vigilance in looking after your crops will pay dividends in stopping problems getting out of hand, and regular inspection will enable you to nip problems in the bud. This section describes a few of the main pests and diseases you are likely to encounter. It's not an exhaustive list – this book is not large enough for that – but it will give guidance on the main problems to watch out for. See also Keeping plants healthy, pages 60–61.

Pests

It sometimes feels as if growing your own food is something of a battle when you are confronted by the array of potential pests that may attack your crops. However, it needn't be like that. Keeping plants healthy (see pages 60–61) outlines many ways to avoid problems. However, the most effective way to keep pests under control is by vigilance. Spending time looking over your crops as you work on the allotment will enable you to prevent pest numbers building up and becoming an infestation. The control measures listed here for the pests described will help you to keep them in check without having to resort to an arsenal of chemicals.

Aphids

Aphids (*Aphidius spp.*) are small, soft-bodied insects, up to 5 mm (¼ in) long, that feed on plant sap. They are usually known as greenfly or blackfly, although their colours also include red, orange, yellow, brown and black. Females can give birth when only a week old, so numbers can quickly get out of hand. They attack a wide range of vegetables, fruit, herbs and flowers, and it is the young shoots at the growing tips that are most susceptible to attack – they become distorted when affected. Pick or rub off with your fingers any infestations and grow attractant flowers to encourage predators, such as ladybirds and hoverflies. Pesticide sprays to use to eliminate aphids include those based on insecticidal soap, pyrethum and rapeseed oil.

Cabbage root fly

Cabbage root flies (*Delia radicum*) lay their eggs at the based of plants of the cabbage family. The white, legless larvae, up to 8 mm (¾ in) long, then feed on the roots

Right Colonies of all types of aphids can build quickly and ruin a crop.

causing the plant to wilt. Damage is most noticeable in spring and early summer. Cover plants with fleece or fine mesh immediately after planting, or place collars, made from bits of old carpet underlay or the purchased eqivalent, around the bases of the plants.

Carrot fly

Carrot flies (*Psila rosae*) are small, shiny, black flies. They lay eggs in the soil around carrots, parsnips and parsley from spring onward. The creamy white larvae, up to 1 cm (½ in) long, feed on the plant roots. The first symptoms on young plants appear as reddening of the foliage and stunted growth – though you may see nothing until you harvest the roots, which will have tunnels in them where the larvae may be visible. Cover with fleece or fine mesh immediately after sowing and keep the plants covered. Carrots and parsley are the most susceptible crops, but carrots sown in June should avoid first generation attack. Sow seeds thinly to avoid having to thin seedlings, as flies are attracted by the smell of bruised foliage.

Caterpillars

Caterpillars of various kinds affect a wide range of crops, but the most common one is the caterpillar of the cabbage white butterfly (*Pieris brassicae*). Symptoms are ragged holes eaten into leaves – black excrement may be left behind. The culprits are often

Left If left to get out of control flea beetles on plants can often leave the leaves looking like net curtains.

found on the underside of leaves. Some cabbage white butterflies attack roots, while others bore holes into the stems or feed on fruits and berries. Caterpillars are the larval stage of moths and butterflies and they vary in size and colour. These pests are most easily controlled by picking them off the plants. Wasps and birds are good caterpillar predators.

Codling moth

Lydia pomonella are small, brown-headed, white-bodied caterpillars that affect apples and pears from mid- to late summer. The females lay their eggs on fruits from early to midsummer and larvae hatch out two weeks later. The larvae then tunnel into the core of the fruit making them inedible. Control codling moth by using pheromone traps, which attract male moths preventing them from mating with female moths. Earwigs and blue tits are good predators.

Currant blister aphid

Currant blister aphid (*Crytomyzus ribis*) are pale yellow aphids and are found on the undersides of plant leaves from spring to early summer. They overwinter as black eggs on currant and gooseberry bushes and hatch out as the flower buds break in spring. Red- and whitecurrants are most susceptible, but blackcurrants and goose-berries are also be affected. When attacked, leaves develop conspicuous blisters in spring and early summer. To control the aphid, pick off any infected leaves; grow attractant flowers to encourage predators;

and don't overfeed with nitrogen, as this causes soft, sappy growth that is more susceptible to attack.

Flea beetle

Flea beetles (*Phyllotreta* spp) are small, shiny, black beetles, about 3 mm (⅛ in) long, that jump when they are disturbed. They hybernate in plant debris and attack the whole range of brassicas, including radishes, turnips, Chinese cabbage and rocket. In spring and summer the adults eat small holes in the leaves – a heavy attack is likely to kill seedlings or stunt the growth of larger plants. Control flea beetle by encouraging seedlings to grow quickly, and never let plants go short of water. Sowing under fleece or fine mesh will help to prevent damage. If necessary, keep the plants covered throughout the life of the crop. Alternatively, get a piece of wood and smear it with grease. Run this over the tops of the plants, and the beetles will jump up and stick to the grease.

Potato cyst eelworm

Heterodera rostochiensis and *H. pallida* are a common pest of the potatoes on the allotment, particularly where a crop rotation has not been used. The tiny eelworm survives in cysts in the soil that may last for 20 years or so. The main symptoms are poor growth and cropping, and pinhead-sized cysts can be seen on plant roots in the summer. Avoid build-up of the pest by using crop rotation (see pages 24–5). Grow resistant varieties where the pests occur.

Left Caterpillars can strip a plant of leaves literally overnight.

Organic control

Prevention, avoidance and quick action are the keys to organic pest and disease control. Use a range of methods and techniques, and as you learn more about how pests and diseases work you will become more confident in dealing with them.

Pest- and disease-resistant cultivars of fruit and vegetables don't confer immunity to a particular problem, but they are a useful part of an organic strategy.

Predators and parasites, from hedgehogs to hoverflies to ladybirds and microscopic worms and fungi, will appear naturally on your allotment when you garden organically. Encourage them to stay by introducing water (see page 40), growing flowers or by leaving a small corner of your plot uncultivated as safe cover. And of course, by not using pesticides that could kill them.

Biological controls are natural predators and parasites bred for release to control a specific pest. Most are used indoors or under cover where suitable temperatures can be maintained, but some can be used outdoors. Most useful for allotments is the microscopic nematode worm that is watered on to the soil to kill slugs.

Physical barriers, such as horticultural fleece, fine mesh netting and bird netting, can keep small and large pests at bay. There is also available a range of foliar sprays, including liquid seaweed, that are said to give some resistance to pests and diseases.

In controlling pests and diseases organically be vigilant and remove any pests or diseased plant material as soon as you spot them – wear rubber gloves if picking off caterpillars is not for you.

There will be times when it seems impossible to grow certain fruits and vegetables successfully with almost everything conspiring against you, but be persistent and you will be amply rewarded.

Slugs and snails

These familiar pests attack a wide range of plants – almost no plant is immune. Both are soft-bodied, slimy creatures with snails having a distinctive hard shell. Slugs vary in colour from pink to black and from a few millimetres to several centimetres. Most slugs feed above ground but the keeled slug feeds below ground and is a major pest of potatoes. Both slugs and snails feed mostly at night as they prefer damp conditions. Symptoms show as irregular holes in leaves, roots and stems; seedlings can also be eaten. There is no one method of control, so use a range of techniques around plants especially when they are young. Hand-pick at night or use various traps baited with beer or milk, ensuring the lip of the container is raised slightly above soil level. Using bran or comfrey leaves around plants will also give some control. Also, encourage natural predators, such as frogs, beetles and hedgehogs. Alternatively, you can purchase a biological control product that is watered on to the soil; this contains microscopic predatory nematode worms.

Wireworms

These are thin, shiny and brown larvae of the click beetle. Wireworms (*Agriotes spp.*) make small holes in carrots and potatoes, and will also attack the roots of brassicas, beans, beetroot and onions. Cultivate the soil in winter to expose the larvae for birds to feed on. Lift potatoes in early autumn to reduce damage.

Diseases

Diseases can often be more difficult to control than pests. While it is possible to use physical barriers to prevent pest attacks, diseases are usually spread by spores in the air or by fungi in the soil, which makes them more difficult to control. By growing crops well and providing plants with everything they need – water, air, light and appropriate nutrients – they will grow strongly and be able to withstand attacks from diseases. Grow disease-resistant varieties wherever possible. A good rotation plan will also prevent diseases building up in the soil.

Blackcurrant reversion

The minute big bud mite is thought to spread blackcurrant reversion (*Cecidophyopsis ribis*) – a viral disease. The symptoms show as fewer indentations in the leaves, and diseased leaves are also darker and narrower than normal. Fruit yield is reduced. In winter remove buds showing signs of big bud (large, swollen buds) and remove any distorted leaves early in spring.

Remove and dispose of badly infected bushes. Always buy plants certified as being disease-free.

Broad bean chocolate spot

Botrytis fabae thrives in damp and overcrowded conditions. Spores can overwinter on plant debris. Symptoms show as round chocolate-coloured spots that develop on leaves, stems and pods, and in severe infections the spots may eventually merge until the plant is totally blackened and dies. To control broad bean chocolate spot provide ample space between plants and grow in well-drained soil. If the disease is a regular problem avoid sowing in autumn – spring-sown plants are better able to recover than plants infected later in the season.

Celery crown rot

Myocentrospora acerina, a fungal disease, thrives in damp soils that are rich in organic matter. Infection occurs through wounds and this disease can survive in the soil for many years. The symptoms show as stunted growth and yellowing leaves; dark lesions develop on roots, leaf stalks and the crown of the plants; and plants being stored develop a red tinge on the leaves. To control, grow celery in well-drained soil and use crop rotation (see pages 24–5).

Leftt The chocolate coloured spots of this broad bean chocolate spot are easily recognizable. Pick off any infected leaves.

Left *Botrytis* or grey mould can ruin
an entire crop of strawberries. Good
circulation will reduce the problem.

Clubroot

Plasmodiophora brassicae is a serious, soil-borne fungal
disease that affects all brassicas, and can remain in the
soil for up to 20 years. It occurs more often on acid than
alkaline soil. The spores are easily spread, transported
on equipment and shoes, as well as on plants. Plants
wilting on hot days, stunted growth and red tints on
foliage are all symptoms of clubroot. Roots swell up
and plant growth becomes stunted reducing crop yields.
Raise your own plants or buy transplats from a reputable
source. Lime soil if it is acid, and use four-year crop
rotation. If clubroot is present on your allotment, raise
plants in pots to give them a head start before planting
out. Dispose of infected plants, but don't put them on
the compost heap.

Grey mould

The *Botrytis cinerea* fungus survives in the soil and on
plant debris. The spores are spread by wind, rain and
soil splashes, and infection is usually through a wound.
Most living or dead plant material can be infected
including flowers, fruits and leaves. A fluffy grey-white
mould grows on infected areas. If the stems are infected
the growth above the infection will wilt and die. Good
hygiene, removing all infected parts as you see them,
will help to control or prevent grey mould. Also, make
sure plants have plenty of space around them for good
air circulation.

Leek rust

Leek rust, *Puccinia allii*, which is spread by spores that
survive on crop debris, is often worse on nitrogen-rich
soils or where levels of potassium are low. If soil is high
in nitrogen, grow leeks in another part of the plot, as
high nitrogen encourages soft disease-prone growth.
Leeks, onions, garlic, chives and other allium species
can all be infected. In summer reddish-orange pustules
appear on leaves and stems. In a severe attack whole
leaves may turn yellow and die, therefore reducing plant
size and crop yield. The disease declines in the cooler
weather of autumn. To control leek rust improve soil
drainage and check nitrogen and potassium levels –
adjust as required. Use crop rotation with preferably
four or five years between growing on a particular patch.
Control weeds and give plants plenty of space when
planting to allow good air circulation.

Powdery mildews

Mildew is caused by a range of fungi including *Erysiphe*,
Sphaerotheca and *Podosphaera spp*. These fungi are most
prevalent when the soil is dry, but the air is humid and
stagnant. Symptoms appear as white fungal growths on
foliage. Mildews can affect other parts of plants, but
their location depends on the type of mildew and the
plant species. Affected plants can split and soon begin
to rot. Severe attacks can reduce growth, cause dieback
or even kill off the plant. To avoid mildews keep plants
adequately watered and look for resitant cultivars. Prune
out infected areas in spring and summer. Mulch plants
to retain moisture in the soil and don't apply a lot of
nitrogen-rich fertilizers or organic matter, which
encourage soft growth that is especially vulnerable.
Plants can be sprayed with sulphur, but this may harm
the leaves.

Onion white rot

Onion white rot (*Sclerotium cepivorum*) is caused by a
soil-living fungus that can survive in the soil for around
15 years. It affects all member of the onion family
(*Alliaceae*). Autumn-planted onions and garlic are most
at risk from mid- to late spring when the soil warms up.
Plants suddenly start to die, older leaves turn yellow,

roots become stunted and rot off, and seedlings keel over. The base of plants develop white, fluffy fungal growths that later produce black fruit bodies (*Sclerotia*). These fall off on to the soil where they persist. To control onion white rot remove and burn infected plants as soon as possible, and don't grow members of the onion family on the same piece of ground for at least eight years.

Silver leaf

The fungus *Chondrostereum purpureum* causes silver leaf, and it shows as a silvery sheen on the leaves. It mostly affects plum and cherry trees, but it can also affect peach, nectarine, almond, apple and pear trees. If you cut through an infected branch of at least 2.5 cm (1 in) diameter the inner tissues will reveal brown staining – other healthy looking limbs will show signs later. Affected limbs can die and fall off, or fail to produce leaves in the spring. Fruiting bodies of a dark, purple-grey colour may also develop on the dead wood. No control is available, but to limit the disease prune susceptible trees in the summer when infection is least likely to occur. Remove and burn any sources of infection including fallen timber. Natural recovery can take place with mild infections.

Potato and tomato blight

Phytophthora infestans is a fungal disease that over-winters on infected potato tubers and plants. It will spread rapidly to new potato and tomato crops in warm, damp conditions. Spores are washed from foliage in to the soil by rain, where they infect the tubers. On potatoes, symptoms show as dark blotches on leaves and stems; white mould can develop on the undersides of the leaves in humid conditions and the whole plant may collapse. Infected tubers decay to a foul-smelling mush, caused by bacterial soft rots. Tomato foliage displays similar symptoms as for the potato, and the stems and green fruits develop dark markings. Fruits begin to rot. Control blight by planting certified, disease-free, seed potatoes. If blight is a regular problem choose resistant varieties. Remove and compost any leaves showing signs of infection, and destroy any potatoes that have grown after being left in the ground after harvest. To control blight on tomatoes remove any leaves showing signs of the disease.

Your allotment year

Spring

Vegetables

Early spring
- Start successional sowing of all salad crops
- Feed spring cabbages with organic fertilizer
- Start sowing peas, beetroot and French beans outdoors under cloches in milder areas – in colder areas leave until late spring
- Sow leeks, Brussels sprouts and cabbages in seedbeds outdoors

Mid-spring
- Cover emerging potato shoots with fleece to protect plants from frost
- Sow spinach beet outdoors
- Plant out shallots, onion sets, potatoes and Jerusalem artichokes
- Plant out peas, spinach and other salad crops started earlier indoors
- Plant asparagus crowns
- Sow sweetcorn indoors or outside under cloches if the soil is warm enough
- Sow maincrop peas, turnips, kohl rabi, carrots, beetroot and Swiss chard for summer crops

Late spring
- Plant out globe artichokes, French beans and onions raised indoors
- Put up canes ready to support runner beans later in the season
- Plant aubergines and peppers under cloches or in cold frames
- Plant out squash and other fruiting vegetables under cloches
- Earth up potatoes
- Place discs of carpet underlay under brassicas to protect them from cabbage root fly
- Put a barrier around carrots or cover them with fleece to protect them from carrot fly

Fruit

Early spring
- Protect blossom of early-flowering trees with fleece
- Finish planting bare-rooted trees and bushes
- Start tying in shoots of briar fruits (blackberries and hybrid berries)
- Feed and mulch all fruit
- Check netting on fruit cages

Mid-spring
- Hand-pollinate blossom if covered with protection
- If forcing strawberries under cloches remove some cloches during the day to allow pollinating insects in

Late spring
- Water newly planted fruit trees and bushes
- Mulch all fruit with organic matter
- Start tying in shoots of any wall-trained fruit
- Put up codling moth traps

Herbs

Early spring
- Sow perennial herbs, such as chives, fennel, sage and thyme, indoors

Mid-spring
- Sow annual herbs, such as basil, borage and dill, indoors; sow in modules and plant out in late spring

Late spring
- Begin to divide perennial herbs, such as chives, lovage and thyme
- Plan and plant a new herb garden

Summer

Vegetables

Early summer
- Continue successional sowing until late summer
- Start planting out tender vegetables, such as tomatoes and sweetcorn
- Transplant spring-sown brassicas
- Transplant leeks sown in seedbeds earlier in the year

Midsummer
- Harvest and store shallots
- Tie in shoots of cucumbers growing up canes
- Sow chicory outside
- Earth up maincrop potatoes
- Begin harvesting early potatoes

Late summer
- Start late sowings of turnips and carrots to harvest in late autumn
- Sow Swiss chard
- Cut the tops off any infected plants
- Sow spring cabbages
- Sow quick-maturing salad crops for a late harvest
- Start lifting some onions

Fruit

Early summer
- Check all fruit netting to make sure birds are not caught in it
- Continue tying in all fruit, where necessary
- Spray aphids with insecticidal soap, if necessary

Midsummer
- Thin fruit clusters after the natural thinning (June drop) has finished
- Watch for sawfly larvae on gooseberries and spray with derris
- Watch for mildew on all fruits and spray with derris or remove infected shoots, if necessary
- Harvest blackcurrants

Late summer
- Start summer pruning of trained fruit
- Peg down strawberry runners to increase stock
- Harvest summer-fruiting raspberries
- Harvest strawberries and cut off any old foliage
- Support heavily laden branches of fruit trees
- Prune plum trees
- Pick early apples for eating
- Harvest briar fruits and cut out any fruited canes
- Plant new strawberry beds

Herbs

Early summer
- Plant out herbs sown in spring
- Begin to harvest fresh herbs as and when required

Midsummer
- Continue harvesting herbs
- Take cuttings of perennial herbs, such as lavender, rosemary, sage and thyme

Late summer
- Begin to dry herbs, such as lavender, sage and rosemary
- Store herbs by freezing in ice cubes

Autumn

Vegetables

Early autumn
- Tidy up rotting leaves and other debris to prevent disease
- Start lifting and storing root vegetables, such as carrots and potatoes, before frosts begin
- Earth up celery and leeks
- Transplant spring cabbages
- Lift and store maincrop onions

Mid-autumn
- As runner beans finish cropping cut off the tops and compost them
- Save some runner bean seeds for next year
- Watch for caterpillars on brassicas
- Plant winter lettuce
- Harvest chicory and store roots

Late autumn
- Force chicory inside and seakale and rhubarb outside
- Cut down Jerusalem artichokes
- Cut down asparagus foliage
- Make sure that netting covering brassicas is secure against birds
- Sow broad beans outside under cloches for an early summer crop
- Protect cauliflowers from frost by bending leaves over the curds
- Remove yellowing leaves of brassicas and compost them
- Complete earthing up celery

Fruit

Early autumn
- Continue to tie in new shoots of briar fruits to their support wires
- Check all tree ties and stakes; loosen ties if they are too tight
- Prune out any diseased or damaged wood
- Finish summer pruning of all trained fruit trees
- Continue to plant new strawberry plants

Mid-autumn
- Cut back fruited shoots of blackberries and other hybrid berries
- Take hardwood cuttings of redcurrants, blackcurrants and gooseberries
- Trim off mildewed shoots of all fruits
- Put grease bands around the trunks of apple and cherry trees

Late autumn
- Pick and store late apples
- Cut back foliage of autumn-fruiting strawberries
- Plant bare-rooted trees and fruit bushes
- If the soil is frozen heel in trees and bushes in a sheltered corner of the allotment plot
- Check fruit in store and remove any showing signs of rotting

Herbs

Early autumn
- Sow annual herbs in pots and keep on a windowsill at home
- Take a risk and sow some annual herbs under cloches or in a cold greenhouse
- Continue harvesting and storing herbs
- Sow some parsley for a winter crop

Mid-autumn
- Continue harvesting herbs

Late autumn
- Lift a few roots of mint and pot up for a winter supply; grow indoors on a windowsill
- Clear away all annual herbs killed by frost and put the remains on the compost heap
- Tidy up the herb area for winter

Winter

Vegetables

Early winter
- Force chicory roots in a warm place
- Test the soil pH (how acid or alkaline the soil is) and add lime if necessary
- Begin winter digging
- Cover a piece of land with polythene to protect it from the worst weather
- Check stored vegetables and remove any showing signs of rotting
- Lift and divide rhubarb

Mid-winter
- Cover a patch of soil with cloches to warm it up for a few weeks ready for sowing outside
- Continue winter digging

Late winter
- Feed spring cabbages with seaweed meal
- Start sowing onions indoors
- Start planting early potatoes under polythene
- Plant Jerusalem artichokes
- Start planting out under cloches early sowings made indoors

Fruit

Early winter
- Start winter pruning of fruit trees
- Continue planting bare-rooted trees and bushes

Mid-winter
- Inspect fruit in store
- In cold areas protect fig trees and peaches with fleece or polythene

Late winter
- Protect flowers on early-flowering, trained fruit trees with fleece or polythene
- Cut autumn-fruiting raspberries to the ground

Herbs

Early winter
- Take root cuttings of herbs, such as comfrey, mint and horseradish
- Tidy herb beds, if not done earlier
- Continue to harvest perennial herbs from summer through winter

Mid-winter
- Take root cuttings as for early winter

Late winter
- Plan a new herb area
- Order seeds of herbs from seed catalogues or herb specialists

Index

Page numbers in **bold** indicate entries in the directory sections.

Garden Organic

Europe's largest organic gardening charity, Garden Organic offers a wealth of expertise on how to grow fantastic vegetables, fruit and flowers in a sustainable way.

Garden Organic is renowned for its educational, social, research and international work. For example, our Duchy Originals Garden Organic for Schools project helps pupils at more than 4,000 schools to grow their own organic vegetables; our research team plays a leading role in helping commercial growers across the UK to adopt organic methods; and our Overseas Organic Support Group funds vital work to help small-scale farmers in developing countries to grow their produce organically.

This registered charity, formerly known as HDRA, is supported by over 30,000 members in the UK and overseas. Membership is open to all. Garden Organic also manages three beautiful display gardens that are open to the public: the charity's headquarters Garden Organic Ryton, Warwickshire; Garden Organic Yalding, Kent; and Audley End Organic Kitchen Garden in Essex (in association with English Heritage).

Garden Organic Ryton is also home to the wonderful Vegetable Kingdom, which offers a fun introduction to Britain's vegetable history, and The Heritage Seed Library that conserves more than 800 old and unusual vegetable varieties.

Much more information about Garden Organic, how to join, and about organic gardening in general, is available at our website www.gardenorganic.org.uk. For further enquiries call +44 (0)24 7630 3517, email enquiry@gardenorganic.org.uk or write to Garden Organic, Ryton Organic Gardens, Coventry, CV8 3LG United Kingdom

* Garden Organic is the working name of the Henry Doubleday Research Association. Charity no: 298104.

Acknowledgements

Although an author's name sits on the cover, there is, in fact, a large team of people involved in producing any book, and I would like to express my sincere thanks to all the people involved with this book. Without their help and encouragement it wouldn't have been completed. There are too many people involved to mention everyone individually and inevitably I would forget, given my bad memory, and leave someone out. However, I would like to thank everyone at Garden Organic for allowing the project to go ahead. Special thanks go to my editor Camilla Davis and all the team at Gaia Books for their professionalism, good humour and for keeping me on the right track. Thank you also for the grateful assistance of Mike Faith, Barbara Davis, Domenico and Maria Pacitto, Vincenzo Romitelli, Ernesto Capocci, George Maslov and all the members of Barriedale Allotment Association, New Cross.

Ian Spence

Commissioning Editor Jo Godfrey Wood
Editor Camilla Davis
Executive Art Editor Leigh Jones
Designer Ginny Zeal
Photographer Laura Forrester
Production Manager Simone Nauerth
Picture Researcher Sophie Delpech

picture credits

Special photography:
© Octopus Publishing Group Ltd/Laura Forrester.
Other photography:
Alamy/Arco Images 132 bottom left, 135 top; /The Garden Picture Library/Sunniva Harte 40; /Holt Studios International Ltd/Nigel Cattlin 49 picture 16, 84, 144, 149; /Niall McDiarmid 31 bottom right; /mediacolor's 136 top; /Mike Stone 44 left. **Andrew Lawson** 147, 150; /Torie Chugg 56, 146; /Designer Sara Wolley 39. **Frank Lane Picture Agency**/Nigel Cattlin 115; /Mike Lane 41 bottom. **GAP Photos**/Jo Whitworth 118. **The Garden Collection**/Jonathan Buckley 13, 17 (pictures 6 & 7); /Liz Eddison 61; /Andrew Lawson 32; /Marie O'Hara 49 picture 18, 88. **Garden Organic** 159. **GardenWorld Images** 151 right; /Dave Bevan 31 bottom left, 151 left. **Getty Images**/Innerhofer 140 bottom. **Harpur Garden Library**/Jerry Harpur 71; /HMP Leyhill, The Garden of Eden, RHS Chelsea, 2001/Marcus Harpur 72. **Ian Spence** 4 bottom centre, 6 bottom left, 8, 60. **Leigh Jones** 4 bottom, 6, 6 bottom centre, 12 left, 48 left, 68, 121, 138 bottom. **Mike Faith** 16, 17 picture 4. **Octopus Publishing Group Ltd** 45 top, 70 right, 78, 107; /Michael Boys 24 left, 24 centre left, 49 (pictures 11 & 19), 79, 98, 119, 120 bottom left, 125, 137 bottom, 138 top; /Jerry Harpur 49 (pictures 5 & 9), 76, 89, 120 top centre, 120 top left, 120 bottom right, 120 bottom centre, 122, 123, 126, 127, 128, 130, 148; /Marcus Harpur 10, 26, 27, 42, 44 right, 132 top left, 134 top, 143 bottom; /Neil Holmes 24 right, 49 (pictures 3, 4, 6, 12, 13, 14, 17), 70 centre, 74, 81, 82, 86, 90, 94, 97, 99, 109, 111, 120 top right, 124, 140 top; /Peter Rauter 17 picture 3; /Howard Rice 49 picture 2, 63 centre, 63 bottom, 102, 104, 117; /Steve Wooster 63 top; /George Wright 24 centre right, 49 (pictures 8 & 10), 92, 93, 100, 110, 129, 131. **Photolibrary** 77, 87, 132 top centre, 132 bottom centre, 134 centre, 134 bottom, 135 bottom, 136 bottom; /Melanie Acevedo 141 top; /Anne Green-Armytage 139 top; /Pernilla Bergdahl 139 bottom; /Richard Bloom 116; /Chris Burrows 49 picture 15, 114; /Brian Carter 31 centre left, 31 centre right; /Christi Carter 112; /Chassenet 80; /Stephen Hamilton 48 right, 103; /Francois De Heel 85; /Heyligers 19 left; /Martin Jacobs 83; /Chris Jones 132 bottom right, 141 bottom; /Linda Lewis 91; /John Mccammon 108; /Reporters 142 top; /Howard Rice 49 picture 7, 105, 106; /Janet Seaton 143 top; /J. S. Sira 113; /Rachel Weill 132 top right, 137 top; /Jo Whitworth 101.